Letters from the Rocky Mountain Indian Missions

Letters from the Rocky Mountain Indian Missions

•

Father Philip Rappagliosi

Edited by Robert Bigart
Translated from the Italian by Anthony Mattina
and Lisa Moore Nardini
Translated from the German by Ulrich Stengel

University of Nebraska Press : Lincoln
and London

Library of Congress Cataloging-in-Publication Data
Rappagliosi, Philip, 1841–1878.
Letters from the Rocky Mountain Indian missions /
Philip Rappagliosi ; edited by Robert Bigart ; trans-
lated from the Italian by Anthony Mattina and Lisa
Moore Nardini ; translated from the German by Ul-
rich Stengel.
p. cm. Includes bibliographical references and index.
ISBN 0-8032-3953-X (cloth : alkaline paper)
ISBN 978-0-8032-4614-0 (paper : alkaline paper)
1. Indians of North America - Missions - Rocky Moun-
tain Region. 2. Rappagliosi, Philip, 1841–1878 - Corre-
spondence. 3. Jesuits - Missions - Rocky Mountain
Region - History. 4. Jesuits - Rocky Mountain Region
- Correspondence. I. Bigart, Robert. II. Title.
E98.M6.R23 2003 266´.278´08997–dc21 2003044798

TO DR. K. ROSS TOOLE,
whose belief in a graduate student
made this work possible.

"Every Indian is a friend and brother to me,
because God has put them
in my charge with all his goodness and mercy . . ."

Philip Rappagliosi, S.J.   *March 3, 1874*

Contents

ILLUSTRATIONS

Editor's Preface

The letters of Father Philip Rappagliosi, S.J., provide one of our most detailed sources on Salish Flathead Indian life in the Bitterroot Valley, Montana Territory, in the middle 1870s. The descriptions of everyday Salish activities are especially valuable, as most other sources emphasize unusual events over the normal daily routine. The documents also relate valuable information about the lives of the Jesuit missionaries, the different Salish tribes of the Flathead Indian Reservation, the Canadian Kootenai Indians, the Piegan Indians, and the Métis Indians in Montana Territory. The St. Mary's Mission letters are the richest sources, presumably because everything was new and exciting to the novice missionary and he had more letter-writing time as he could do little church work until he learned to speak Salish. Because he could speak neither English nor Salish, Rappagliosi's observations may have been less influenced by biases he would have picked up if he were getting information orally from the local white population.

As a window on Montana Indian life in the 1870s, the letters are a valuable historical source on these Indian communities just before the collapse of the buffalo herds. Extensive and traumatic social and economic changes were coming with the eradication of the buffalo herds in the early 1880s. The world Rappagliosi described would soon be dramatically changed by dislocation and the pain of starvation. These tribes had only about ten years before they would have to almost totally rebuild their economic life.

This translation uses Indian or Native to translate the Italian selvaggio. Selvaggio could have been translated as savage, but the English savage has a much more negative connotation than does the Italian word. There was no indication in the letters that Rappagliosi intended disdain by using selvaggio, and the editor and translators believed that

Indian or *Native* was a more accurate English translation. For the most part, the translation preserves the capitalization and punctuation of the Italian originals. Some punctuation changes were made, however, to clarify the meaning of obscure passages.

The first publication of most of these letters was assembled in 1879 by an unidentified editor, who also included a biographical sketch by Joseph Guidi, S.J., and a letter from Jules Decorby, O.M.I. From that publication – Filippo Rappagliosi, S.J., *Memorie del P. Filippo Rappagliosi, D.C.D.G., missionario apostolico nelle Montagne Rocciose* (Rome: Bernardo Morini, 1879) – we have included Rappagliosi's letter about entering the Jesuits (*Memorie*, 33-34) and his letters about his trip to America and about the missions (*Memorie*, 51-149). Footnotes in this collection that were taken from the 1879 edition are followed by the attribution "1879 editor." Letter 17 was published in English in the *Annals of the Propagation of the Faith* (Dublin, Ireland) 40, no. 21 (Jan. 1877): 231-36. Letters 20 and 26 were originally published in German in the *Katholischen Missionen* (Freiburg, Germany) 4 (1876): 173-74, 197-98. The titles given to letters 1, 17, 20, and 26 were added in this edition; other letters carry the titles given them in the 1879 edition.

ACKNOWLEDGMENTS

This volume of Rappagliosi's letters would not have been possible without the support of K. Ross Toole, Hammond Professor of History at the University of Montana in the 1970s. Ross's faith in and support of his graduate students was an important contribution for many beginning historians.

Father Clifford Carroll, S.J., of the Oregon Province Archives at Gonzaga University gave permission to copy the Italian version of the *Memorie*.

Father Thomas E. Connolly, S.J., of Sacred Heart Mission, DeSmet, Idaho, generously translated the Latin expressions in the book. Dr. Linda Frey of the University of Montana Department of History assisted with the translation of a French letter from the Oblate Archives in Rome.

Salish Kootenai College provided two faculty research grants from the Bush Foundation that allowed the editor to pursue a number of sources in the Gonzaga University Libraries in Spokane, Washington, and paid for the translation of the German letters from *Katholischen Missionen*. Father Clifford Carroll, S.J., and Brother Ed Jennings, S.J., were gracious hosts at the Oregon Province Archives and courteously answered many requests both in person and by mail. Dr. Anthony Mattina, Dr. Dale Johnson, Dr. H. Duane Hampton, and George Price of the University of Montana, Missoula; Dr. Joe McDonald and Ron Thierrault of Salish Kootenai College; the late Dr. John Ewers of the Smithsonian Institution; and the late Dr. Patrick Morris of the University of Washington-Bothell have generously taken the time to read the manuscript and offer suggestions and ideas. The Flathead Culture Committee of St. Ignatius, Montana, and the Kootenai Culture Committee of Elmo, Montana, were also kind enough to read the manuscript.

I cannot express enough my thanks to all the people who so freely assisted with this project. I hope they will approve of the results. Any mistakes, however, are the responsibility of the editor alone.

The Cultural and Historical Landscape

In 1841 Father Pierre DeSmet, S.J., led a small band of white Christian missionaries who established St. Mary's Mission in the Bitterroot Valley of what is now western Montana. The mission was in the homeland of the Salish Flathead Indians. Earlier in the century the Salish Flatheads had adopted a number of Iroquois Indians who had come west with the fur trade. The Iroquois had provided valuable manpower to help the Salish fight the westward-moving Blackfeet tribes who contested the right of the Salish to hunt buffalo on the plains east of the Continental Divide. The Iroquois had also told the Salish about the spiritual power of the white people – Christianity.

The fight with the much more numerous Blackfeet Indians and their allies and several epidemics of smallpox and other previously unknown contagious diseases had seriously eroded Salish military power. In addition to the manpower problems, the Salish had a long and tenuous supply line for guns, ammunition, and metal products. Most of the white traders came from the southern Canadian plains or up the Missouri River. Both of these military supply routes were regularly threatened by the Plains tribes, who objected to the arming of their traditional enemies in the Rocky Mountains.

With these military pressures endangering the physical and spiritual survival of the Salish, they joined their allied neighbors, the Nez Perce Indians, in inquiring about the spiritual powers of the whites. These inquiries, or "delegations," to St. Louis during the 1830s quickly became popular legends in the United States. The first missionaries to respond were the Protestant Christians, but they did not wear black gowns or use the incense, bells, and vestments that had impressed the Iroquois with Catholic worship. The Protestants continued west to the lower Columbia River Basin. Finally, in 1840, Father DeSmet was designated to survey the prospects for Catholic missions among the Rocky Mountain tribes. The Salish were receptive to his teachings, and DeSmet returned to St. Louis to assemble the missionary party that was to establish St. Mary's Mission in the Bitterroot Valley.

DeSmet was a Jesuit, or member of the Society of Jesus, a Roman Catholic religious order that had been active in American Indian missions for centuries. In 1814 the pope lifted a fifty-year suspension of the order, and the Jesuits slowly began to rebuild. The Rocky Mountain Indian missions were to become a major enterprise for the reestablished order. DeSmet, an effective publicist and fund-raiser, spent most of the years after 1840 in St. Louis, raising support for the chain of missions among the Salish Flathead, Pend d'Oreilles, Coeur d'Alene, Blackfeet, and other Indian tribes.

Some of the missions faltered due to intertribal hostilities, cultural conflicts between the priests and their Indian parishioners, and environmental problems such as flooding, but by January 1874, when Father Philip Rappagliosi, S.J., arrived at St. Mary's Mission, the missions had grown into a chain of substantial establishments with churches, farms, shops, and schools.

In the 1870s, when Rappagliosi worked at St. Mary's, political and economic changes that would impact the lives of the Salish people and their neighbors were sweeping across the United States. In the years after the U.S. Civil War the country entered a period of dramatic expansion. The late 1860s brought many white miners to the valleys of the northern Rockies. These hordes of miners were followed by white farmers and entrepreneurs. The great expansion of the white population in the area increased competition for resources. White farmers plowed up traditional Salish root- and berry-gathering sites, and white hunting dramatically reduced wild game populations. In 1873 Rappagliosi was able to use the Union Pacific Railroad to travel only as far as Utah Territory, but by 1883 the transcontinental Northern Pacific Railroad was completed through the Yellowstone and Clark Fork Valleys in Montana.

In the 1860s the U.S. government was preoccupied with the Civil War and Reconstruction and paid little attention to the northern Rockies. The government Indian agents were usually more concerned with personal profit than with helping or interfering with the daily lives of the Salish. In the 1870s, under President U. S. Grant's Peace Policy, Indian agencies were assigned to Christian mission societies. The Protestant churches received many agencies where Catholic missionaries had been established for years, resulting in considerable sectarian conflict. The Flathead Agency was assigned to the Catholic Church, but the Blackfeet Agency was assigned to the Methodists. The Protestant agents tried to exclude or impede the work of the Catholic missionaries at St. Peter's Mission. The problem of corruption among government Indian Service employees continued despite the church control of agencies. In 1871 the U.S. House of Representatives forced an end to the practice of making treaties with Indian tribes, which were ratified only by the Senate. Instead, the United States would enter into agreements with Indian tribes that would require the approval of both houses of Congress.

Most of the Rocky Mountain tribes with whom Rappagliosi worked were Plateau culture area tribes who by 1874 were using horses to seasonally hunt buffalo on the Plains. Although the Salish Flathead, Coeur d'Alene, Nez Perce, Pend d'Oreilles, and Kootenai Indians all lived west of the Continental Divide, they made regular buffalo hunting trips to the Great Plains. The hunts usually started in the late fall, and the hunters returned to the western valleys in the spring. Sometimes another, shorter, hunt was made in the summer. The Blackfeet tribes were part of the Plains culture area and engaged in continuing warfare with the western tribes in an unsuccessful attempt to keep them out of the Plains buffalo grounds.

In addition to hunting buffalo, the Rocky Mountain tribes also relied on hunting game such as deer, elk, moose, and rabbits in their western homeland; gathering roots, berries, and other plants seasonally; and fishing. For some of the far western tribes, fishing was as important as the buffalo hunt. During this period the tribes still lived in buffalo-skin tepees that could be easily moved to follow game herds or to travel to root and berry sources. The horse was the key to the mobility of the tribes and was critical to both subsistence and warfare. The tribes Rappagliosi visited were not involved in the major Indian-white wars of the 1870s, but they were engaged in intertribal skirmishes and horse raiding. All the Rocky Mountain tribes Rappagliosi met, except the Kootenai and Nez Perce, spoke a dialect of Salish. The Nez Perces spoke a Sahaptian language, and the Kootenais spoke another unrelated language. The Blackfeet, who had invaded from the east about a hundred years earlier, spoke an Algonquian language. In 1877 the Métis were recent immigrants from the east who were attracted by the buffalo herds in the Milk River Valley, which was then on the Blackfeet Reservation. The Métis spoke French, English, and Cree, another Algonquian language.

As a Jesuit, Rappagliosi was part of a hierarchy that stretched back to Rome. In the 1870s each of the missions, such as St. Mary's, was headed by a superior who was responsible to the superior general, the head of the entire Rocky Mountain Mission of the Society of Jesus. The superior general was under the father provincial of the province of Turin, Italy. In turn, the father provincial reported to the father general, or head of the entire Society of Jesus. The father general was directly under the pope.

Rappagliosi's letters describe many details of everyday Indian life at the missions in the 1870s, but he wrote very little about the political and social changes that were then beginning to sweep over these tribes. This selective vision could have been the result of Rappagliosi's inability to speak English when he arrived at St. Mary's or the hesitancy of either Rappagliosi or the 1879 editor of the letters to include political material.

The groups he visited ran the range from those who had almost been displaced by the invading white population to those who had been only minimally impacted:

- The Canadian Kootenais had not yet been invaded by white settlers in interior British Columbia, but they suffered from the increasing shortage of buffalo on their seasonal hunts to the Plains.

- The Piegan Indians were still the most dependent on the buffalo. They had no agriculture or cattle ranching on which to fall back. They suffered further as neighboring enemy tribes moved onto their reservation to hunt the shrinking buffalo herds.

- The Pend d'Oreilles Indians on the Flathead Indian Reservation were protected from white settlement and hunting on the reservation, where they had begun developing farms and cattle ranches. They had been greatly impacted by the reduction of the buffalo on the Plains and the increased white competition for game and gathering sites off the reservation in western Montana.

- The Salish Flathead Indians in the Bitterroot Valley had no protection from white competition. In addition to the shortage of buffalo east of the mountains, a growing white population in the Bitterroot Valley was over-harvesting game and occupying grazing and gathering sites. As Rappagliosi observed, some of the Bitterroot band were developing their farms for year-round support and were expanding their cattle herds.

- The Métis were the most affected by the growth of the white population. Largely the result of intermarriage between the local Indians and the white and Indian fur trade employees, they had previously lived by farming combined with seasonal buffalo hunts. Displaced by English immigrants and attracted by the profits of the buffalo-robe trade, they switched to full-time buffalo hunting. The Métis included mixed-bloods and remnant Indian groups from the southern Canadian plains and the Dakotas.

Each Indian community that Rappagliosi described was in a different social and political situation in the 1870s. Among these differences ran common threads of reduced resources and increased competition from invading white settlers. The following discussion considers the particular situation of each group in the order that Rappagliosi met and described the group in the letters.

The Salish Flathead Indians in the 1870s

The little band of about 350 Salish Flathead Indians gathered in a small village around St. Mary's Mission in the Bitterroot Valley of western Montana. The Indian community was being buffeted by political, economic, and environmental changes, but Father Rappagliosi said little of the changes affecting the tribe.[1]

In the previous twenty years this band had entered into two agreements with the U.S. government, and the government had not fulfilled the terms of either. The 1855 Hellgate Treaty provided for establishing a school, hospital, and various craft shops and supplying manufactured goods in return for the Salish Flatheads giving up most of western Montana. The treaty was not ratified by the government for almost four years, until 1859. The required survey to determine whether the Bitterroot Valley should be reserved for the Indians was pro forma at best. Much of the annuities received were useless because the goods purchased were foodstuffs and clothing rather than the agricultural tools, guns and ammunition, kettles, and tinware that the Salish Flatheads needed. The coffee in the first annuities had been salvaged from a sunken riverboat. Other portions of the annuities were stolen while in transit or at the agency. Many of the annuity goods seem to have been used in running the agency rather than distributed to the tribe. In commenting on one of the many fraud cases against Flathead Agency employees in the 1870s the U.S. attorney for Montana, M. C. Page, claimed in 1876: "That the Government has made ample provision for them [the Confederated Salish and Kootenai Tribes] and that they have been mercilessly robbed of the benefits of such provision, are matters of such notoriety that they admit of no question."[2]

No government school was established, although some salaries were paid to the St. Ignatius Mission schools. The government agency was established in the Jocko Valley, about fifty miles north of St. Mary's, which was too far away to be of much use to the Bitterroot Valley Salish.

In 1872 Congressman James A. Garfield, the future president, was sent to the Bitterroot Valley to negotiate with the Salish. Garfield may have taken the assignment because he preferred the isolation of Montana over the embarrassment of campaigning for the reelection of President Ulysses S. Grant.[3] In Montana Garfield was able to negotiate an agreement with two of the three Salish Flathead chiefs, providing for houses and additional services to aid those who removed to the Jocko (Flathead) Reservation. The descriptions of the houses built by a politically qualified contractor suggest that they were almost uninhabitable. Congress did not appropriate most of the money needed to fulfill the 1872 Garfield agreement, so funds appropriated for the 1855 treaty obligations were diverted to pay for costs under the 1872 agreement. The 1872 agreement led to the division of the Salish Flathead band in the Bitterroot, with less than 100 following Chief Arlee to the reservation and the remaining 350 remaining in the Bitterroot Valley. In addition, the Garfield agreement was published with an "X" indicating that Charlo, the chief of the Bitterroot Salish, had signed. The text of the published report stated that Charlo did not sign, but many Montana whites were selective readers and claimed that Charlo had agreed to remove from the Bitterroot Valley. Chief Charlo and most of the band, consequently, did not trust the government's promises.

Other changes affecting the tribal community were also troubling. The number of white settlers had increased dramatically in western Montana. In 1870 there were 20,595 white people in the territory, most of whom lived in the gold-mining camps. Missoula had about sixty-six buildings and 300 white residents in 1870, but the nearby mining camps on Cedar Creek, near present-day Superior, had an estimated 3,000 white residents. Some sources suggest that 450 white residents lived in the Bitterroot Valley in 1869, which would have been about equal to the Indian population of the valley. The increasing white population meant growing competition for pasture, wild game, and gathering sites.[4]

Although the Salish Flatheads maintained friendly relations with most local whites, some of the white leaders in western Montana seemed to encourage friction between the communities in hopes that conflict would expand the local white economy. In the late 1870s the mining camps declined, and the white population and white economy contracted. Some Missoulians saw a military post and its local spending as the best means to assure that Missoula did not become a ghost town. In the 1870s the *Weekly Missoulian* was fanning the embers of friction between the races. The newspaper claimed that the local whites were in immediate danger from lawless Indians despite sixty years of evidence to the contrary. The Salish Flatheads had been valuable allies of the whites and were proud of having never fought or killed any white people. Ignoring the history of peace, in 1874 the *Weekly Missoulian* editorialized that "The Indians of this part of the Territory have been nominally friendly for a long time, . . . [but] Peace is abnormal to the Indian. . . . The blaze of Indian warfare will surely light up the valleys of this country in time."[5] Finally, in 1877, Fort Missoula was established in the face of continued Salish assurances of peaceful intent.

The Missoula County government was grinding toward bankruptcy in the late 1870s and desperate to expand its tax base. It unsuccessfully attempted to force whites who had married into the tribes and were living on the Flathead Reservation north of Missoula to pay property taxes. The county also attempted to make the Bitterroot Salish pay taxes on their farms and stock. An 1870 report found thirty-five farms averaging about twelve acres each and six hundred cattle, one hundred hogs, and eleven hundred horses belonging to the band.[6] The attempt to force the Salish to pay taxes on their remaining lands infuriated Charlo, who delivered a famous speech on the subject in 1876, which was recorded in the *Weekly Missoulian*:

Yes, my people, the white man wants us to pay him. He comes in his intent, and says we must pay him — pay him for our own — for the things we have from our God and our forefathers; for things he never owned and never gave us. What law or right is that? What shame or what charity? The Indian says that a woman is more shameless than a man; but the white man has less shame than our women. Since our forefathers first beheld him, more than seven times ten winters have snowed and melted. Most of them like those snows have dissolved away. Their spirits went whither they came, his, they say, go there too. Do they meet and see us here[?] Can he blush before his Maker, or is he forever dead? Is his prayer his promise — a trust of the wind? Is it a sound without sense? Is it a thing whose life is a foul thing? And is he not foul? He has filled graves with our bones. His horses, his cattle, his sheep, his men, his women have a rot. Does not his breath, his gums, stink? His jaws lose their teeth, and he stamps them with false ones; yet he is not ashamed. No, no; his course is destruction; he spoils what the Spirit who gave us this country made beautiful and clean. But that is not enough; he wants us to pay him besides his enslaving our country. Yes, and our people, besides, that degradation of a tribe who never were his enemies. What is he? Who sent him here? We were happy when he first came; since then we often saw him, always heard him, and of him. We first thought he came from the light; but he comes like the dusk of the evening now, not like the dawn of morning. He comes like a day that has passed, and night enters our future with him.[7]

In 1877 when Chief Joseph and the Nez Perce Indians fled through the Bitterroot Valley, Charlo and the Salish refused to join their traditional allies in fighting the whites. Charlo and his warriors insisted that the Nez Perces not harm the white settlers in the valley.

As aggravating as government perfidy and the friction with the surrounding white community must have been, the decline of the buffalo herds was even more threatening to the future economic independence of the Salish community in the Bitterroot. In 1874 when Rappagliosi arrived at St. Mary's, the buffalo on the Plains were still adequate to feed and cloth the Salish, but some may have started to wonder about changes in the movements of the herds and the more frequent need to travel farther to harvest enough buffalo to supply the tribe.

The Salish leadership in the Bitterroot Valley actively promoted expanded agriculture to protect the tribe's well being and independence. During the 1870s most Salish extended families engaged in some farming and ranching. The leadership also struggled to prevent hostilities from erupting between the Salish and white communities. Efforts to keep the peace were successful, but the economic efforts failed in the face of adverse weather, insects, and white competition. Finally, in 1891, Charlo agreed to move his impoverished band to the Jocko Valley on the Flathead Reservation.

ST. MARY'S MISSION

Both the deathbed visions of a young Salish girl and the priests' agricultural plans pointed toward a mission station in the Bitterroot Valley. The year before the priests arrived in 1841, a dying young Salish girl named Mary had a vision of the Virgin Mary and prophesied that the house of prayer would be built in the Bitterroot Valley. The missionaries dreamed of St. Mary's Mission becoming the nucleus of a Salish community governed by Christian – specifically Roman Catholic – principles. The mission was to be the center of an Indian community supported by agriculture, without the traditional Salish gambling games and with marriages and other aspects of life organized along European patterns. The missionaries wanted to establish a religious agricultural community among the Salish that was modeled after the famous seventeenth- and eighteenth-century Jesuit-operated reductions, or settlements of Paraguayan Indians.[8]

Their custom of hospitality and desire for supernatural aid in their long, bloody struggle with the Blackfeet led the Salish to show the early white religious leaders special deference. The Salish were interested in limited farming but not in giving up their buffalo hunting-based economy. They were willing to abandon their infrequent polygamous marriages and have Christian marriage ceremonies. They were happy to accept the protection of baptism and were even willing to stop public gambling. But the priests' efforts to impose a new theocratic lifestyle based on long hours of agricultural labor and religious instruction were largely rejected.

The priests' willingness to share this new power with the Blackfeet, the mortal enemies of the Salish, added to Salish disenchantment. The ethnocentrism of the missionaries finally proved too much for the Salish. The priests, having lost the support of the Salish and fearing the increasing Blackfeet raids in the valley, closed St. Mary's Mission in 1850. The buildings and the location were sold to John Owen for use as a trading post.

While they rejected the missionaries' attempt to make them into European farmers, the Salish did not want to give up the spiritual power of Christianity. They continued the Christian prayers and ceremonies and visited St. Ignatius Mission after it was moved to the Mission Valley in 1854.

In 1866 St. Mary's was reestablished as a center of worship for the Salish, but without the grand designs for a self-contained theocratic community. A new church building was built that same year. By 1874 the St. Mary's Mission consisted of a log chapel about nineteen by twenty-two feet, two rooms for living quarters attached to the rear of the chapel, a blacksmith shop, and a few farm buildings. It was but a shadow of the dreams of Father DeSmet in 1841, but it served a central role in the Salish community in the 1870s. Rappagliosi's letters describe much about the daily activities at St. Mary's during this period.

The mission continued until 1891, when Charlo and the last of the Salish band removed to the Flathead Reservation to the north. After 1891 the church was visited by nonresident priests to provide church services for the local white residents.

The Flathead Indian Reservation

The turmoil of change during the last quarter of the nineteenth century was only beginning in 1875, when Rappagliosi was at St. Ignatius. The choices the tribes faced were not easy. Surely most tribal members would have preferred to maintain the buffalo-based economy. The debate must have started already in 1875, but Rappagliosi mentions nothing of it. While not as detailed as his letters from St. Mary's, his St. Ignatius letters provide some intriguing glimpses of worship and death at St. Ignatius Mission and of Chief Arlee and his small band in the Jocko Valley in 1875.

The Pend d'Oreilles and Kootenai Indian communities on the Flathead Reservation faced pressures similar to those on the Bitterroot band of Salish Flatheads. The reservation Indian community was, however, larger and more protected from white competition, and it received some assistance from the mission and agency. The Indian people on the Flathead Reservation survived the wrenching changes of the late nineteenth century and largely maintained their economic and social independence until the early twentieth century brought new and even more dangerous problems.[9]

In 1875, when Rappagliosi was stationed at St. Ignatius Mission, the future must have looked grim to the reservation Indian leaders. As already noted, the main economic base for the tribes was becoming increasingly less dependable. The shrinking buffalo herds were ever farther away from the reservation, and the herds that remained attracted many hunters from enemy tribes. White settlers were becoming more common in the valley bottoms off the reservation. The whites competed for game and pasture and occupied some traditional gathering sites.

The promised economic aid from the government was of little use. Shops sometimes did not exist at all, and those that did were often without tools and equipment. The agency employees were not qualified craftsmen and spent most of their time doing clerical work, herding, or farming for the agency. Since the agency was in the Jocko Valley, it could provide little assistance to the Indian community, whose members lived mostly in the Mission Valley to the north. In 1875 the Indian population in the Jocko Valley was limited to a few government employees and the small band of Salish Flatheads under Chief Arlee who had recently removed from the Bitterroot Valley. In addition, the constant turnover of agents and other government employees made it impossible for even those few who were competent or well intentioned to have a positive impact.

Arlee was the second chief of the Salish in the Bitterroot, and less than one-fifth of the Salish followed him to the Flathead Reservation. In 1875 the band consisted of 81 people.[10] Under the agreement negotiated by Congressman James A. Garfield in 1872, Chief Arlee and his followers received five thousand dollars per year for ten years, which was supposed to be enough relocation money to assist the entire Bitterroot band.[11] Chief Arlee and his family occupied the old Flathead Agency building and farm, and the agency was moved to another site in the Jocko Valley. According to a November 13, 1873, inspection report by J. W. Daniels, Arlee was not satisfied with the new house built for him. Daniels observed that the new houses the government constructed were made of green lumber that had "shrunk so bad that they are not fit for human beings to live in."[12]

To add to the turmoil, in 1874 Agent Charles Shanahan attempted to divert school salary funds to build homes for the Salish Flatheads who had removed from the Bitterroot Valley with Chief Arlee. Congress had not provided the funds promised in the 1872 agreement, so Shanahan attempted to use the salary money for teachers promised in the 1855 treaty to pay for part of the Garfield agreement obligations. The missionaries complained to Washington DC, pointing out that the government had not paid for the school buildings as provided for in the treaty and had contributed little to the cost of maintaining the pupils. Paying the teachers' salaries was the closest the government came to fulfilling the treaty provision for a school. Shanahan's decision was reversed by the Office of Indian Affairs in Washington, and he soon lost his job.

On November 1, 1874, Arlee wrote the president complaining that Peter Whaley, the new Flathead agent, was "governed by priests" and charging that the St. Ignatius Mission was getting rich from the treaty funds for the school. This was about five months before Rappagliosi's 1875 visit to Arlee that is described in letter 20.[13]

The Indian community on the Flathead Reservation had some advantages over those that remained in the Bitterroot Valley: (1) the Indian population on the reservation was larger, at about thirteen hundred; (2) because the Flathead Reservation was officially recognized, the government did keep white settlers off it, which reduced the competition the tribes faced for resources; and (3) the reservation community had some outside assistance in learning new technologies. The mission schools and shops provided services to the tribal members, and the agency must have occasionally been of some help. The white and mixed-blood farmers and ranchers who married into the tribe played an important role in spreading knowledge about ranching and farming.

Most important, however, was the astuteness of the reservation leadership. They pursued a strategy similar to that of Charlo and the leaders of the Bitterroot band, but the reservation leaders actually had the resources to succeed. The Pend d'Oreilles and Kootenai leadership worked to develop new economic resources — ranching and farming – to replace the declining return on hunting buffalo and other big game. The desire of the leadership to maintain the economic independence of the tribes was strong enough to keep the tribes basically self-supporting despite the loss of the buffalo. By 1900 the Flathead Reservation had established a new economy based on ranching, farming, and some wage work. Research by economist Ronald Trosper indicates that at the beginning of the twentieth century the Flathead Indian community was about as well off economically as other rural Montana communities. In other words, the Indian community was not poor until the federal allotment policy forced the tribes to sell much of the reservation land to white homesteaders at bargain rates. After being forced to give up most of their assets at below market prices, they saw their standard of living decline significantly during the first half of the twentieth century.

The tribal leadership on the reservation also worked hard to maintain peace between the Indian and white communities, but this was easier on the more isolated reservation. The agents from 1877 to 1898 – Peter Ronan and Joseph Carter – worked with the traditional leadership in the tribe. The agency police and judges were largely drawn from the traditional leaders. Ronan, especially, relied on the chiefs to help keep order and encourage economic change.

ST. IGNATIUS MISSION

In the 1870s St. Ignatius Mission was a large and bustling establishment, quite a contrast to the quiet backwaters of St. Mary's Mission. The first St. Ignatius Mission was established in 1844 along the Pend d'Oreille River in eastern Washington Territory, not far from Lake Pend d'Oreille. Because the first site was not centrally located and was subject to seasonal floods, the mission was moved in 1854. The new location was in the Mission Valley of western Montana, about seventy miles north of where St. Mary's had been located in the Bitterroot Valley.[14]

In this period St. Ignatius boasted a wood-frame church, a farm, a gristmill, and a sawmill operated by the Society of Jesus and a girls' boarding school and a day school for boys operated by the Sisters of Charity of Providence. In 1875 the girls' boarding school had twenty-eight pupils while the boys' day school had only an irregular attendance.[15] The wooden mission church, constructed in 1864, was forty by one hundred feet with a belfry over one hundred feet tall. Held together with wooden pins, the church was in the Roman style with clerestory, columns, and apse.[16] In the 1890s it was replaced with a brick structure that is still standing.

In the 1870s a village of Indian cabins and tepees surrounded the mission complex. Rev. James O'Connor, bishop of Omaha, visited St. Ignatius in June 1877 and left the following description of the village surrounding the mission:

St. Ignatius is not laid out in streets, owing, I was told, to the fact that the Indians insist on locating their cabins so that they may be able to see the church from their doors. They visit it frequently during the day for private prayer, but when not in it they take great pleasure in being able to look at it. "Where a man's treasure is there also is his heart." The cabins as a general rule are about fifteen feet square, well built of pine logs from the neighboring mountains, and are both clean and comfortable. With the exception of one or two bedsteads, I saw nothing that could be called furniture in any of them. The inmates sit or rather squat on the ground or recline on the robes or skins that serve them for beds. Sacred pictures and crucifixes are fastened to the walls, and kettles and other cooking utensils stand on the open hearths or hang from hooks or andirons. The tepees are furnished or unfurnished in like manner only that in them the fire is in the centre of the floor and the smoke escapes through an opening above it. Outside one of the cabins, women were drying beef or buffalo meat over a slow fire. The meat was boned, cut into long strips and laid on an arch of wooden bars about two feet above the fire. Every cabin and tent had its contingent of savage dogs, who recognizing the habit of the Fathers, allowed us to pass if not graciously, at least unchallenged.[17]

In addition to the two or three priests stationed at the mission, four lay brothers worked there in the mid-1870s. The lay brothers worked on the farm and in the gristmill and sawmill and directed twenty Indian employees.

In the 1880s and early 1890s boarding schools were maintained for both boys and girls, and government aid allowed them to enroll over three hundred students. In the mid-1890s the federal government stopped funding mission schools, and the St. Ignatius schools limped along in decline. During 1875, when Rappagliosi was at St. Ignatius, this expansion and contraction were still in the future.

Of special interest is Rappagliosi's description of the piety of the Salish Flatheads and other Catholic Indians. The descriptions of devout Catholic Christian belief did not, however, necessarily indicate that the Salish agreed that they had to give up their Salish beliefs to be good Christians. The view that religious belief was exclusive and that accepting Christian teachings required the abandonment of Indian religion was a European concept. The traditional religious beliefs of the tribes of the northern Rockies allowed for believers to acquire new spiritual powers to supplement and add to their spiritual growth. From the Indian viewpoint, the addition of Christian beliefs and practices would not require the abandonment of other beliefs that had proved valuable. By the same token, the retention of Indian values and beliefs did not suggest that the converts were insincere in their Christian beliefs. To take the approach of some twenty-first-century critics that the Indian converts were just telling the priests what they wanted to hear runs the risk of projecting the secular society of 2003 back to the 1870s and ignoring the strong current of Salish spirituality both before and after Christianity was introduced.

The Canadian Kootenai Indians

Rappagliosi visited two isolated bands of Kootenai Indians northwest of St. Ignatius Mission in 1874 — the Tobacco Plains and Cranbrook bands. These Indian communities spoke an entirely unrelated language and had an economy that was less dependent on buffalo hunting. After 1874 the Canadian Kootenai were served by priests of the Oblates of Mary Immaculate, a French order of the Roman Catholic Church, working out of St. Eugene Mission near Cranbrook,

British Columbia. The Bonner's Ferry, Idaho, and Elmo, Montana, Kootenai bands continued to be under the Jesuit missions.

The Kootenai Indians in the Tobacco Plains and Cranbrook bands were far less impacted by white competition in 1874 than the Montana tribes among whom Rappagliosi worked. The buffalo may have become a little scarcer, but these bands relied less heavily on Plains buffalo hunts. The Canadian Kootenais used fishing, hunting, gathering, and farming in the Columbia Basin for most of their support.[18] In 1859 Dr. James Hector of the Palliser Expedition observed that the Cranbrook Kootenai band had five hundred horses and ten to twelve cows. About this same time George Gibbs saw wheat planted by the Cranbrook band and wheat, turnips, potatoes, and parsnips raised by the Tobacco Plains band.[19]

The Kootenai Indians must have heard of disturbing developments in surrounding areas. In the late 1850s and the 1860s white gold miners flooded into the Fraser and Thompson River drainages to the west, bringing conflict and intense competition to these neighboring tribes. In the 1870s the first white farmers moved into eastern interior British Columbia, and from the south the Kootenais learned of the surge of white miners and farmers in Montana.

The British Columbia government did not recognize any Indian title to the land and consistently tried to displace the Indian people to make more room for white settlers and land speculators. The Indian groups to the west were allowed small and unproductive reserves, usually being left with considerably less than ten acres per person. Even these reserves were encroached upon by neighboring whites, with no protection from the Provincial Government or compensation.

The Canadian Kootenais saw many of these problems move closer in the 1870s, but few white people had yet moved into southeastern British Columbia. Tensions mounted over the 1870s and 1880s as the province continued to ignore Kootenai land claims and resource needs. In 1887 trouble boiled over and Chief Isadore — whose father, Chief Joseph, Rappagliosi had met thirteen years earlier (see letter 17) — forced the release of a Kootenai man being held in a white jail.

The Kootenai, Kapula, had been accused, on very little evidence, of the 1885 murder of two white miners. The North West Mounted Police moved in to try to mediate the problems but had only limited success. The provincial government did make some minimal adjustments to increase the size of the Kootenai reserves. The basic problem of British Columbia's refusal to respect Native land claims has never been addressed. In the twenty-first century it is still a major problem for British Columbia Native peoples.

The Montana Blackfeet

In the late 1870s the Blackfeet Indians – or, more properly, the Piegan Indians – that Father Rappagliosi visited were still near the height of the Plains Indian culture based on the horse and the buffalo. A little over a century before they had driven the Salish and Snake Indians off the Plains and had acquired horses. The horse proved to be of great military and economic value on the Plains, and during the eighteenth and nineteenth centuries the Blackfeet experienced a flowering of their military power, wealth, and arts and crafts. The horse greatly expanded their ability to hunt the buffalo, which provided the resource base for their economy. The Piegans were one part of the Blackfeet Confederation, which also included the Bloods and the Blackfeet proper, who later settled in Canada. In the early 1850s the Blackfeet Confederacy, then including the Gros Ventres, contained 9,170 people, which was almost seven times the population of the Salish Flatheads and the Upper and Lower Pend d'Oreille tribes combined.[20]

By the time of Father Rappagliosi's visits to their camps, however, the Blackfeet were seeing the beginning of the end of their way of life. The white population expanded rapidly in the Rocky Mountain valleys to the west in the early 1860s, and the massacre of a peaceful Blackfeet band by a U.S. Army force led by Col. E. M. Baker in 1870 largely ended the sixty-five-year military competition with the Americans. Even more ominously, the buffalo herds were shrinking. As noted previously, in the late 1870s the buffalo were largely extinct to the north and east of the Blackfeet country, and many other tribes were moving into the Milk River area to hunt the diminishing resource. Many of these tribes were traditional enemies, and their concentration in the area resulted in increased intertribal warfare. The reduced herds were harder to locate, and periods of hunger became more frequent. Finally, in the early 1880s the herds disappeared, and the Blackfeet and other Northern Plains tribes starved until the U.S. government began supplying regular rations. Later in the nineteenth century the Blackfeet traded land for rations and government assistance in starting farms and cattle herds in the harsh Northern Plains climate.

These were troubling and tumultuous times for the Blackfeet. Father Rappagliosi was only beginning to learn the Blackfeet language, and his letters give few hints that he understood the complicated changes that were leading the Blackfeet to crisis.

ST. PETER'S MISSION

In 1840 Father DeSmet was the first Jesuit missionary to visit the Blackfeet. Father Nicholas Point, S.J., also worked among the Blackfeet during the 1840s. The first St. Peter's Mission was not established until 1859, however, and it was moved several times before it was closed in 1866. The mission was the victim of the increased Blackfeet-white hostility of the period. In 1874 St. Peter's Mission to the Blackfeet was reestablished near the Missouri River between the Sun and Dearborn Rivers after an eight-year closure. The new location was close to Bird Tail Rock, about fifteen miles south of the present-day town of Simms, Montana. As Rappagliosi indicated in his letters, the Blackfeet did not live near the mission. It was just a residence for the priests who traveled with the Blackfeet camps across northern Montana. In 1877 St. Peter's consisted of two small one-room buildings, one of which served as a chapel as well as living quarters for the missionaries.[21]

Reductions in the size of the Blackfeet Reservation after 1878 left St. Peter's Mission off the reservation, and by the same time federal Indian policies had assigned the Blackfeet to Methodist missionaries. In the 1880s the mission was moved several more times and was finally located on the reduced Blackfeet Reservation and renamed the Holy Family Mission. Those Blackfeet tribes that ended up in Canada were ministered to by the Oblates of Mary Immaculate. Only the Piegans in northern Montana were the responsibility of the Jesuit fathers.

A striking aspect of Rappagliosi's letters from St. Peters is the hospitality and courtesy the Piegans showed the missionaries. The Piegans shared their food and lodges with the missionaries. The missionaries were guests in the chief's lodge and were invited to feast where special foods were available, and the Piegans allowed the priests to baptize their children. Even though the Piegans were not Christians, they listened respectfully to the teachings of the priests and were willing to learn the missionaries' prayers and catechism. The Piegans treated their visitors with courtesy and respect and shared whatever they had with their guests.

The Métis

The Métis camp on the Milk River near Frenchman's Creek in north-central Montana represented a unique meld of Indian and white cultures. Descendants of the French, English, and Scottish employees of the fur trade and their Native wives, the Métis had developed a culture that drew on both their Indian and their European heritages. They made up most of the population of the Red River settlement that eventually became Winnipeg, Manitoba, and were the primary source of laborers for the fur trade. In 1870 the Dominion of Canada took control of the Hudson's Bay Company's Rupert's Land claim and the political and economic future of the Métis. A rebellion led by Louis Riel in 1869 and 1870 forced the Canadian government to pass laws to protect Métis land claims, but these laws were not vigorously enforced.[22]

The Métis developed a mixed economy of hunting and agriculture, combining seasonal buffalo hunts to provision the fur trade with part-time agriculture at Red River and other settlements. Problems with land claims and other harassment from English-speaking Canadian colonists made it hard for the Métis to keep their farms. At the same time the growing market for buffalo robes in the 1870s attracted many Métis to year-round hunting. Some abandoned their farms and spent the entire year following the buffalo herds. This economic adaptation was successful during the early 1870s, but by the late 1870s the buffalo herds were diminishing. The Métis hunters had to travel farther to find buffalo, and the hunts were sometimes unsuccessful.

One of the last refuges for the northern Great Plains buffalo was the Milk River Valley in northern Montana. During the late 1870s and early 1880s many Indian and Métis groups gathered there to hunt the diminishing herds. During the summer of 1877 Father Rappagliosi traveled with a group of about 70 families following the buffalo herds in the Milk River drainage. This camp spent the winter of 1877-78 living in huts along the river bottoms in the Frenchman Creek area. The U.S. Army estimated in February 1878 that the camp contained 108 families with 611 people. More Métis arrived during 1878, and in October 1878 the Army estimated that about 300 Métis families were living in the general area.

The camp on the Milk River included a number of Canadian Métis who had been displaced from their farms and many families of American Métis who were members of Chippewa Indian bands in North Dakota. These American Métis families had also followed the shrinking buffalo herds to Montana. The priests of the Oblates of Mary Immaculate had been active in western Canada for many years, and the Métis in the camp were Christian and spoke French. Father Rappagliosi was already fluent in French from his school days and enjoyed the pious reception the Métis gave him.

The Métis camp in Milk River was also a symptom of the traumas that would destroy the basis of Métis life in the Northern Plains: the buffalo population was rapidly imploding, and the U.S. Army and the North West Mounted Police were establishing military control of the region. To postpone disaster, the Métis moved south and west of their accustomed hunting grounds. However, the Milk River was then part of an Indian reservation for the Blackfeet, Gros Ventres, and other tribes.

Another resident at the Milk River camp during the winter of 1877–78 was Father Jean Baptiste Marie Genin, who was to figure in Rappagliosi's story. Father Genin had worked with the Sioux during the 1860s and was adopted as a brother by Sitting Bull. Because Father Genin had traveled freely among the camps of hostile Sioux refugees in Canada after the Battle of Little Big Horn and he and his parishioners had aided the wounded and destitute Nez Perce refugees from the Battle of the Bear Paws in 1877, the U.S. Army was quite antagonistic to Father Genin and the Métis camps in the Milk River area. During November 1878 the soldiers based at Fort Benton forced the Canadian part of the camp to retreat north of the forty-ninth parallel. Father Genin had left for Canada during the spring of 1878.

The American part of the camp moved to the Sun River area off the reservation in April 1878. In 1879 most of these American Métis moved to the Judith Basin and founded the community of Lewistown. With the collapse of the buffalo herds, the Métis in Lewistown turned to ranching and gardening for support.

The Canadian Métis also suffered from the loss of the buffalo and land competition from English-speaking Canadian immigrants. In 1885 the Canadian Métis again revolted against the Canadian government but were quickly defeated. The Canadians did resolve some of the Métis claims, and they gave the Métis land scrip that some were able to use to establish a new way of life based on agriculture. Most, however, became an impoverished underclass, suffering discrimination from English Canadians.

The American Métis from the camp Father Rappagliosi visited established communities across Montana but received only limited and largely unproductive homestead allotments. Seasonal agricultural labor and other laboring jobs barely allowed the Métis to survive. The twentieth-century mechanization of agriculture and economic depression in eastern Montana reinforced their poverty by eliminating many unskilled job opportunities. In 2003 some descendants in the Little Shell Band of Chippewa Indians of Montana were still struggling to receive federal recognition and assistance from the U.S. Bureau of Indian Affairs.

Biographical Notes on Father Rappagliosi

On January 3, 1874, a thirty-two-year-old missionary priest arrived at St. Mary's Mission in the Bitterroot Valley with an innocent energy and contagious enthusiasm that was soon noticed by the Salish parishioners. Father Philip Rappagliosi's optimism and dedication comes through readily in his letters. The Montana missions and Indian camps lacked many of the physical comforts Rappagliosi was used to in Europe. His letters treat these changes as challenges rather than ordeals. Both Fathers Joseph Guidi, S.J., and Rappagliosi were at St. Peter's Mission in 1877, but their descriptions of the Blackfeet camps were quite different. Guidi saw "the monotony of savage life, the food, and the annoying insects which swarm in the Indian lodges"; Rappagliosi, in contrast, described the openness of the Blackfeet to the missionary teaching and their hospitality and willingness to share what they had.[23] This positive attitude must have been noticed by the Indians who welcomed him.

Obviously Rappagliosi thoroughly accepted the Christian missionary ideology. He had no doubt about the superiority of Christianity, and specifically Roman Catholic Christianity, over any other religious value system. His international exposure made him more open-minded about the value of other cultures than most white Americans in the 1870s, but he was not a cultural relativist. Other cultures had value only to the extent they could accommodate Judeo-Christian teachings.

Father Rappagliosi saw the Indians as children: children he loved, but not his intellectual equals. This attitude could have stemmed from both a feeling of European cultural superiority and a mindset that saw him as a father figure (priest) relating to his children (parishioners). In any event, Rappagliosi was a man of his times.

Readers who want to evaluate him by the moral values of the twenty-first century will be disappointed.

Rappagliosi was born in Rome on September 14, 1841, to Agnese and Carlo Rappagliosi. Very little information is available about his parents.[24] Father Guidi, who knew the family in Italy, stated that the parents were "remarkable for their piety." Rappagliosi's obituary in the *Helena Daily Herald* referred to "respectable parents." Two twentieth-century Jesuit historians, presumably relying on oral traditions in the order, indicated that the Rappagliosis were a "noble family" (Bischoff) and a "wealthy and noble family" (Schoenberg).[25] The Rappagliosis are not listed, however, in the standard reference on Italian nobility.[26]

After attending a Jesuit school at Tivoli, Italy, a small hilltop town near Rome, young Philip entered the Society of Jesus in 1856 at age fifteen. The long period of Jesuit training began with two years as a novice at Rome. This was followed by two years studying rhetoric. When he finished with his course in rhetoric, he was forced to complete two years of his philosophy studies in France due to the wars among the Italian states that culminated in the unification of Italy in 1861. He completed his philosophy course, with honors, at the prestigious Roman College or Collegium Romanum — now known as the Pontifical Gregorian University — which was started in 1551 by St. Ignatius Loyola, the founder of the Society of Jesus. Rappagliosi then taught at the Roman College and began his studies of theology. After completing the theology studies, he did his tertianship, or his third year as novice. He was finally ordained in the Society of Jesus on December 17, 1870, at Laval, France, when he was twenty-nine years old.

In January 1871 he was in Laval when it was threatened by the Prussian army during the Franco-Prussian War. Rappagliosi and the rest of the Jesuits fled west, away from the front. He found refuge in a Jesuit house in Vannes on the Atlantic coast of Brittany. In spite of these brushes with the turmoil that was sweeping Europe as Germany and Italy coalesced into nation-states, most of Rappagliosi's time was spent in study and teaching — spiritual preparation and preaching. He seems to have developed a reputation among the Jesuits for piety and competence.

Poised to enter the church establishment and having already taught at the Roman College, in 1873 the young Father Rappagliosi was offered a professorship of rhetoric. In 1872, however, his friend Father Guidi had left for the Rocky Mountain Mission in America. These missions to the Indians were under the Turin Province of the Society of Jesus. Rappagliosi felt a call to work in the Indian missions rather than the colleges of Europe.

Father General Peter Beckx, S.J., accepted Rappagliosi's request to be assigned to the Rocky Mountain Mission. As an indication of Rappagliosi's position in the church, the father general personally escorted the new missionary to an audience with Pope Pius IX just before Rappagliosi departed Rome.

The letters reprinted here describe Rappagliosi's trip to Montana Territory in 1873 and his arrival at St. Mary's Mission in the Bitterroot Valley on January 3, 1874. While at St. Mary's in 1874, he studied Salish and English and wrote a number of delightful letters to his family. These letters convey his excitement and enthusiasm for his work at the mission. Fortunately they also describe many of the details of daily life among the Bitterroot Salish in the 1870s and the interactions between the Salish and the missionaries.

In August 1874 Rappagliosi and Father Joseph Bandini, S.J., traveled to Canada to visit the Canadian Kootenai Indian bands. A letter describing this trip was published in several European Catholic periodicals and is also included here.

For the first half of 1875 Rappagliosi was assigned to St. Ignatius Mission among the Upper Pend d'Oreilles Indians in the Lower Flathead River Valley. Fewer letters are available from this period, presumably because Rappagliosi had learned enough Salish by that time to perform his duties as priest. One letter describes Rappagliosi's efforts to mend relations between the missionaries and Chief Arlee, chief of the Salish Flathead Indians who had recently moved to the Jocko Valley.

Between mid-1875 and his death on February 7, 1878, Rappagliosi was assigned to St. Peter's Mission among the Montana Blackfeet. This work involved almost constant traveling to proselytize the unconverted Blackfeet. It was a dramatically different assignment from ministering to the already converted Salish Flathead and Pend d'Oreilles Indians. This new assignment also involved learning another Indian language.

The shrinking buffalo herds brought other Native groups to the Blackfeet Reservation in the 1870s. Among these groups were French-speaking Métis bands from Canada and North Dakota, who were devout Catholics. Rappagliosi spent several of his trips on the Plains with the Métis, and during the winter of 1877-78 he got involved in a conflict with a controversial former Oblate priest, Father Jean Baptist Marie Genin.

On February 7, 1878, Rappagliosi died in the cabin of Alexander Weekly (a.k.a. Wilky) in the Métis camp on the Milk River. Rumors of foul play circulated after his death, but no evidence has surfaced to explain his demise. There was some evidence that Rappagliosi had health problems even before that winter, and his conflict with Genin could have added to the stress. Appendix B offers a more detailed discussion of the questions surrounding Rappagliosi's death.

Father Philip Rappagliosi was the third son of Carlo and Agnese Rappagliosi to die in less than a year. He was buried February 17, 1878, in Helena, Montana Territory.

Letters from the Rocky Mountain Indian Missions

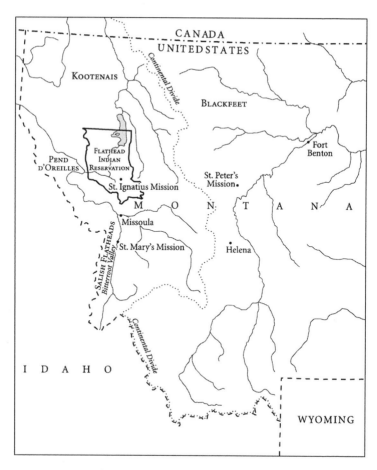

Father Rappagliosi's Missions during the 1870s.

Calling to the Society of Jesus

Tivoli, August 17, 1836 [*sic*, should be 1856]

Dearest Parents,

During the Novena of the Assumption of Our Lady I entreated her with my question, entrusted beseechingly my matter to her and now I write to tell you what she has directed me to do.[1]

First, I am determined not to wait for a year, or even until the end of the fall vacation, to carry out what God has let me know that I should do immediately. It might seem to you that in so doing I want to go against your wishes. Anything else you order, I am ready to obey; but in this matter I must obey God, rather than my parents. Please realize that this decision of mine, however unexpected to you, has not been made without considerable thought. First I cannot wait such a long time, because I see clearly that God wants me, and he wants me now. Second, if I were to come to Rome and spend more than a year there to test my vocation – and my vocation has already been tested repeatedly – you know well how dangerous this could be for me; could I not lose my vocation with so many temptations? Do not think that my vocation is insincere simply because I fear I might lose it, the Lord himself could take it away from me were I to delay so long.

As far as my health, it certainly isn't such that I couldn't adapt to the strict regimen of the novitiate – in fact I have recovered considerably. I hope you can see how sober my request is, and give me the pleasure (I ask for no other) to be able to join the Society before the end of September. Write me a letter where you let me know that you are happy that I should join the Society before the end of September. As for my coming to Rome, I will come, but with the agreement that I should be a novice before October. You can decide the date of my departure from Tivoli when you come here for the reward [graduation] which will take place on the twenty-ninth of this month. I hope you will grant what I ask – knowing your piety I can't expect otherwise.

Pray for me and send me your blessings.

Your most devoted son Philip.

[2]

The Call to Be a Missionary

Tronchiennes, September 8, 1873 (Birthday of Mary)[1]

P. C.[2]

Most beloved parents, brothers, and dearest relatives.

May the grace and love of God be always with us.

With this letter I send you news that might, naturally, bring you pain, but also brings consolation in life, and greater consolation in death!

Merciful God, in spite of my shortcomings and sins, has decided to choose me as an instrument of his glory, and of the salvation of many lost souls. This is how things went.

Already for two years I have felt a most insistent call to the missions, and in particular to the missions of the Rocky Mountains in North America. Surely you remember several letters that I wrote, when I was in France, about the good deeds performed by the missionaries in those places so without spiritual guidance and so in need of it. But this wasn't something to rush into. Only after a long wait, after many prayers to God that he might let me know his will, after many requests for advice to the father of my soul, I finally decided to let my superiors know of this calling, leaving that decision entirely up to them as interpreters of the will of God. On the day of St. Ignatius, a little over a month ago, I wrote to Rome, both to the Father Provincial, and to the Reverend Father General.[3] Before my letters arrived in Rome, the Father Provincial let me know the plans he had for me. Later I found out that he received my letter in Rome on the

same day I received his here. I was ready for any decision, ready only
to do the will of God.

While, as I said, I was in Mons giving spiritual exercises to the
members of that College, a letter from Rome arrived.[4] Without opening it I knew it was from the Father Provincial. I read on my knees,
as if to feel what God wanted from me. For your consolation I send
you an exact copy of this letter, and you will see all the reasons we
have to thank God.

Rome, August 30, 1873.

Reverend Father in Christ,

*After several days of deliberation the Father General has decided to accept
the request that your Reverence made regarding the missions. It seems that
this is truly the will of God because, almost simultaneously you made your
request, and Propaganda made a heartfelt plea to the Father General on behalf of those lost souls, having heard this, I gave an account of the plans
that I had had for your Reverence; but I added that I have no intention to
go against the higher plans of divine Providence, and I put the matter into
the hands of our Father [General].[5] I suppose that you will receive from him
news [of the decision] and pertinent details.*

*For now I rejoice about this second calling that the Lord has given you, a
calling that, if not greater, is certainly rarer than the first. And the Lord will
add to this calling the necessary aids for your Reverence to be his coworker in
the salvation of those derelict souls. It is now time to open our hearts, to great
wishes and sublime hopes; people who know nothing about eternal life are,
perhaps, predestined to go to Heaven through the door that your Reverence
will open for them. Such are the plans of God!*

*With all my respect, and one with your Holy Sacrifices, I remain in Christ
the lowly servant of your Reverence,*

Pietro Ragazzini S.J.

The day before yesterday, just back in Mons from Tronchiennes,
I received the Reverend Father General's letter. O how good the
Lord is!

I send you an exact copy of this, or rather an exact translation since the original is in Latin. You will see the kind of letter this is, and how merciful and generous the Lord our Father is.

Rome, September 2, 1873

Reverend Father in Christ.

I read your letter of July 31st with great pleasure and immediately I felt inclined to support those pious wishes that one could see were inspired by Heaven. All of the missions, but especially the Rocky Mountain Mission, are of greatest concern to me, both because we are summoned there with urgent calls, and our priests, many of whom are overworked and old, cannot fill all needs, and because it is in that Mission that we can reap the richest fruits for the greater glory of God.

Nevertheless, I did not want to settle the matter on the spot. I questioned the Reverend Father Provincial, who had been thinking of sending your Reverence elsewhere, but did not completely rule out releasing you to those missions, where I am confident that you will work to great advantage, yours and that of others.

Then I wrote, to the Reverend Father Provincial of Turin so that he may consider your Reverence released to him for the Rocky Mountain Mission, and send you there with others when he wishes.

In the meantime I give thanks to God. I congratulate your Reverence and that mission. I hope for the best. My dear Father, I bless you with all my heart. Remember me in your prayers.

Peter Beckx S.J.

Consider, if you please, these two letters word for word, as I have done, and tell me if there isn't reason to be thankful to God. You are blessed, as God now asks for further proof of your faith, another sign of the love you have for your faith, another sign of the generosity with which you have already released your son to God. If you could enter my heart you would be able to see that it understands the pain that you must now, naturally, feel. But you would also see the eagerness and the happiness with which I obey God's call, and you could only say: "Son, go where God calls you."

This letter will leave today, day of Mary's birth, I entrust it to the Holy Mother. Only God knows how much I pray for you. I am conflicted about your feelings, yet I find comfort; in the knowledge that you too will be able to be stronger than your pain. Therefore be comforted. This letter (and the one in which I informed you of my vocation for the Society) will be one of our greatest consolations in life and in death.

As you can see from the Father General's words, nothing about the journey has been finalized, and I do not know what month it will take place. It is unlikely that it could be before November.

I have shared with you these two letters, in order to comfort you. I do not let everyone in on the details – they don't need to know. Those who do know, how they do envy me!

God is good, and his ways marvelous!

And you cry? . . . I do know that now you must cry, but these tears do not displease God: they are a natural reaction, but the heart will accept. Oh, we bless God eternally, we bless him in happiness, we bless him in pain, we bless him in life, we bless him in death!

I thank you Lord, that with your call I and my loved ones gain strength! I am at your service. Bless my family and me.

God's grace! We are so generous with God.

Affectionately as always

Philip of the Society of Jesus

P.S. As you hold this letter in your hands I am praying for you. Do pray as well, and then write to me.

[3]

On the Same Topic

Tronchiennes, Exaltation of the Holy Cross 73[1]

P. C.

Dearest Parents.

Last night I received Dad's letter of the tenth of this month. I thank you for your good wishes. The Lord accepts your wishes and blesses them. He blesses them, not always according to our ideas and wishes, but much better. God knows what he is doing, and from above he sees the many and varied strands of human events, and he steers and guides each toward his glory and our eternal life.

By now you must have received a second letter dated the eighth of this month that I wrote to Uncle Andrea. I know this letter must have hurt you, because it hurt me. God's will be done! This is the thought that gives me and you the strength to go against nature.

Going back to what you wrote, you can imagine how I felt reading those words. If you ask your heart how you feel about me, you'll know how I feel about you, and you will understand the effect your letters have on me. But it doesn't matter: Give vent to your feelings, tell me that I don't love you, tell me that I am heartless. The sacrifice wouldn't be a sacrifice if it were not accompanied by all of this. I have anticipated all this! . . .

From my second letter, you will have understood how everything went: you will have seen how, in this matter as always, the superiors have been the instrument of divine Providence. They felt they were being led by a hand, and unanimously agreed to *God's highest will.* These are their very words.

I am still at Tronchiennes where, for now, my only duty is to wait for the orders of obedience, and to pray to God on your behalf and mine for the fulfillment of his wishes.

I haven't yet received a letter from the Reverend Father Provincial of Turin so things stand as when I wrote to you on the eighth.

Mother, Father, don't cry unless you do so to thank God that he has chosen me for the honor of sacrificing myself entirely for his glory. Be the worthy parents of one who has been called to the Apostolate! Let the firmness of your principles and the strength of your faith show above the ugliness of nature.

I pray that God gives to your souls a drop of that consolation that he gives to those who want to sacrifice themselves exclusively for his love. This morning I celebrated the Holy Mass for you. It is not randomly that God decided that you should have brought me into this world on this day. Everything, everything for the Lord!

Enough today. As you can see I had nothing new to add, but I wanted to write because my poor heart, especially these past few days, feels what you feel! God will take care of the rest.[2]

Bless me.

Your most affectionate Son

Philip S.J.

[4]

Travels in England

Liverpool. November 13, 1873

P. C.

Dearest Parents and relatives.

In Tronchiennes I received your dear letter dated the thirtieth of October. I am happy to hear that you are all well and I am gratified that you are happy and accepting of God's will. All things turn on this earth, pivot around this.

Brother Melchers, recently returned from Aix la Chappelle and Cologne, met up with me in Belgium.[1] From Tronchiennes both of us went to Ostend which is a Belgian port, and from where we sailed for England. In the beginning the sea was calm, but soon it showed us some of its tricks. My stomach, thank goodness, remained settled in those ups and downs and I didn't throw up.[2] My companion also made the trip without getting sick. This is not inconsiderable luck. The entire journey we were on deck watching the spectacles of the ocean; one moment it opened up as if to swallow us and then, as if to make fun of us, lifted us up again on new crests. After six hours, with the help of the Lord, we arrived safely at Dover, and from there we went by train to London where we were greeted by Fathers who overwhelmed us with their attention. We stayed in London for three days waiting for news of our Irish companion. Finally we found out his name, Father O'Flinn, and the place where we would meet him, at Queenstown, which is in the path of our journey since the steamboat that goes from Liverpool to America stops at Queenstown, an Irish port.[3] As soon as we found this out, we left London for Liverpool, arriving there after about seven hours on the train. In Liverpool we have a nice College and a beautiful Church. The Fathers received us with the usual kindness and attention. The College is called *St. Francis Xavier* which is also the name of the College in New York! It is a good omen for missionaries who leave Liverpool. St. Francis Xavier sends them off and receives them.

Besides us three Jesuits, there is someone from the American College of Louvain with us, and we are fortunate to share a room with four first-class berths.[4] We each paid 262 francs, and not the more than 500 that I had written before.

I see that many people are praying for us because God is protecting us in a thousand ways; up to this point we haven't had even the slightest problem on this long journey. The greatest part is still ahead, so you will continue to pray even more. . . .

Goodbye my beloved ones: The ship leaves today at two: tomorrow we should arrive at the Irish port from where we will set forth across the Atlantic for New York. If you want to write to me in St. Louis before I write you, I would be pleased. God willing I will write to you as soon as I reach New York. Yesterday I saw the ship, LE CELTIC, that will take us across. If you could only see how huge it is![5]

Goodbye, Goodbye. I have no more time: I must leave.

May God keep you healthy and look over you in all circumstances. Bless you in every way. We must put our hearts and hopes only in him. We are now apart for our love of him: may he be our comfort and our reward.

I embrace you with all my love.

Your most loving son and affectionate relative

Philip Apostolic Missionary, S.J.[6]

[5]

Departure for America

Irish Sea, November 14, 1873

P. C.

Dearest Parents and relatives.

As I wrote from Liverpool, our ship has to stop at the Irish port of Queenstown before crossing the Atlantic. I will take advantage of this opportunity to mail this letter from Ireland, by giving it to one of the passengers who disembarks there to be mailed from there.

I am writing to you while at sea and I am enjoying this opportunity to be with you because nearly all the passengers are either American or English, and I don't know whom I would be speaking with. I've only found an Irish family, all of whom are Catholic, with whom I was able to converse a bit in French. Besides I'm not bored by this silence because the very view of the sea is sublime and enough to occupy my time. And, I have several books to read during the days of the journey. In addition, I must accustom myself to solitude, and not seek personal comforts, but only the glory of God and the salvation of the souls [in my charge].

We left Liverpool yesterday evening. A steamboat came to pick us up at the shore and took us to the Celtic in the middle of the port, for it was too large to come to the shore. Four or five Fathers accompanied us to the Celtic and then returned to shore. They were of great help to us.

We have a nice room with four beds on the ship, so the four of us will be together, that is a young German who is going to Canada to study and become a priest, Brother Melchers, myself, and Father O'Flinn whom, God willing, we will pick up at the Irish port.[1]

If you could only see how splendid and magnificent these English ships are, you wouldn't believe that you are at sea, but rather on land in a mansion with rooms furnished as well as the nicest first-class waiting rooms at railroad stations. For example, I am writing this letter in a handsome room furnished with sofa, rugs, mirrors, a piano, and heaters, in sum the nicest of furnishings. This doesn't mean that a bungalow on land isn't preferable. At the moment the sea is calm, and you can see I am able to write sufficiently well. I'm not sure that it will be so every day. In any case, we are in the hands of the Lord for whose love we have undertaken this enterprise. There are more than 60 passengers besides 160 emigrants and a crew of about 60. Many more people will embark at Queenstown.

I hope that you have received all of my letters and that you are well.

9

For now you must be patient and wait until I arrive in New York, and then wait for my letter to reach Rome.

Goodbye for now: I pray very much for you, and offer my everything to God on your behalf as well.

Pray for me: I embrace you with all my heart.

Yours always

Philip, Apostolic Missionary.

[6]

Transatlantic Crossing and Arrival in New York

Atlantic Ocean, November 15, 1873

P. C.

Dearest parents and relatives:

Last night as we stopped at the Irish port, I had a letter mailed to you. I hope you have received it. We were at the Queenstown port only an hour. There we again took a good look at the land knowing we won't be able to see it for many days.

We are now crossing the Atlantic, today the sea is rougher than yesterday, but you can see that I can still hold pencil and paper. Here at sea, I have very little to tell you that might interest you. We see nothing but ocean and sky and we move however the waves care to carry us. May these waves flatten and let a poor missionary cross, who wants to rush to the help of the poor Indians! It will be as God wishes. The cabin mate who boarded yesterday at Queenstown knows only English. The four of us have no common language, it's a comedy: I speak Latin with him [the Irishman]. Brother Melchers wants me to speak Italian so that he can then translate for our third companion in German; this way *after five minutes* the four of us understood what we wanted to say to one another, that the sea is calm, everything is okay, it could be worse, but that it would be better still if we had land under us. As you can imagine this is our most important topic of conversation, as we are traveling upon nothing but some planks, no matter what illusion the paint and the decoration give us. Nevertheless, except for some nausea that keeps us from eating, for the moment we are getting along fine. It seems to me that the nausea of the passengers is arranged by God for a good reason; to make us understand that the best foods in the world aren't worth anything without the desire to eat them. They put in front of us delicious dishes that should tempt us to overeat, but even the most gluttonous are unable to. It is difficult to write on this unsteady table!

I forgot to tell you about an incident that demonstrates how God protects us. We had left Liverpool and had come aboard the *Celtic*. As the *Celtic* was leaving the port, a small steamboat approached us bringing orders not to. The reason was the thick fog that surrounded us; visibility was poor, we couldn't leave without risking collision with other vessels. This was at four o'clock in the afternoon on the thirteenth. We waited until eight o'clock. Then the Captain gave orders to leave. A few moments later we were stopped again; it was impossible to proceed without danger. We dropped anchor again and spent the night like this. The morning of the fourteenth, at about three o'clock we set forth even though the fog hadn't lifted much. Later we learned that we had avoided an accident. An American ship had stopped in front of us for the same reason. Our ship, already moving, was headed straight for the American ship and the Captain couldn't have seen it. The Captain himself told us that when he finally saw it he had enough time to stop and so we were safe. We arrived at Queenstown at ten o'clock in the evening and we left one hour later.

November 16 (Patronage of Holy Mary)

Today, Sunday and feast day of the Madonna, I had the great pleasure of celebrating the Holy Mass. I celebrated it in my, or should I say our, room, with Father O'Flinn's assistance. Oh, what a great moment, what a great day this is, to be able, in the middle of the Atlantic, to offer the immaculate Host to God and to pray for you, for my companions, for the Church, for the Society. The Captain would have allowed me to celebrate Mass in a larger place, but the sailors were busy cleaning everywhere, and it was not possible. Besides, there are very few Catholics traveling with us: a German fellow, three Spaniards, and a few poor Irishmen, among the emigrants. I hope we can do it next Sunday.

After dinner the Captain allowed Father O'Flinn to preach to the Catholics. The Protestants also gathered together for Sunday service. The Captain had had a notice put up, and a bell was rung.

Friday, November 21

We have had bad weather ever since Sunday evening. On Monday the sea was absolutely terrible about nine o'clock, but it was even worse on Tuesday after lunch when, from two o'clock until eleven o'clock in the evening, there was a terrible storm! I saw what a monster the sea can be! On Wednesday we had a bit of respite, but still the sea was too agitated and I found it impossible to write. Thursday was the same. Today it's quite an effort to write because the rocking goes on. The winds have a hurricane force. We hope to arrive either Sunday evening (the twenth-third) or Monday morning (twenty-fourth). So we wish. For seven days we haven't seen land, only infuriated waters and cloudy skies. Let all be done for the glory of God and the good of the souls. Father O'Flinn and my other companion, Mr. Roettger, are fine and they behave as real sailors; they have never lost their appetite, but are probably the only ones on the ship to do so. Even the strongest and the most courageous have in the last few days given up. Monday and Tuesday very few took a meal. At every meal I have eaten just enough to survive. When we get to New York, God willing, we will rest, and stay with our brethren. I will write to you again from New York. Meanwhile I am writing this letter so I can mail it as soon as, with the help of God, we land. That's it for today: everything and everyone is bumping around.

Saturday, November 22

The Lord pitied us: we truly needed some rest. Yesterday at about five in the afternoon the wind diminished and the sea began to calm down. After so many stormy days we could finally walk about the ship and on deck without having to hold on to every rail or rope within reach. The night was tranquil and we slept very well. Thanks be to God. It is now ten thirty in the morning and the sea is still calm; this is a true pleasure; not even the first two days was it so calm. How long will it last? Leave that up to the Lord. Just now the sailors are shouting and they are changing the position of the sails; apparently the winds have changed. Now I will go to see which sails are up.

Before I forget, I hope that when, with the help of the Lord, I get to New York, you will know it soon: at least I have made arrangement to give you this reassurance; here is how:

In Liverpool I found out that every ship that arrives at New York telegraphs to Liverpool that it has arrived, and that announcement is printed in the newspapers. So I asked someone there that as soon as he had learned that our ship, the Celtic had arrived, would he write to a Father in Belgium, a good friend of mine, and would he be so kind to telegraph to Rome. In this fairly inexpensive way, you will know that I have arrived safely only three or four days after the fact, and without having to wait for this letter, and you can thank God that he has protected me during this voyage so dangerous in this season. Maybe tomorrow we will see land, that is, some islands just before arriving in New York. The last days we have seen very few ships (in all five or six), a whale did some jumping in front of us, and a few large dolphins were chasing us. And then sea and sky, sky and sea.

Saturday, 4 o'clock P.M.

The good weather is lasting; everyone has come back to life. The hope of an imminent landfall, the mild weather, and the calm sea are three things that make us happy after many days of stormy seas and after a violent squall that lasted several hours. Everyone says that we will arrive at New York tomorrow night, but very late, and the passengers won't be allowed to disembark until Monday morning. If this is what happens, I will set foot on land on the first day of the Novena of St. Francis Xavier. It's he who wants to receive me. I remember last year how much I prayed during this same Novena to know the will of God about this holy enterprise. Blessed be this great apostle who designed to take care of this insignificant servant of his. With this letter you will receive a card with the drawing of the magnificent ship that has taken me to America. You can see how big and beautiful she is; we have seen how strong it is, as it withstood so many days of battering. The four masts that support the sails are made of iron. But what is all of this at sea: the sea laughs at it as it would at a piece of straw, and such a large ship is not enough to reassure us. You should have felt how, especially those hours on Tuesday, the furious waves shook her and made her lean to every side, one minute lifting her over mountainous crests, and the next minute hurling her down a deep trough. But today the sea is calm, and she glides majestically across the water; and the sight of this immense blue plain is like a spell. Nevertheless I would prefer beholding it from the shore, never trusting this calm. The sea is fickle, and changes in a moment especially during this season. Let us hope that it stays so until we land, and not think about how it's been. It feels a thousand years since I've had a foot on land: let us hope the Lord will soon grant us this wish. In New York we will rest well among our brothers at the College of St. Francis Xavier.[1] Even here in the new world I find our Society and embrace other religious brothers.

I don't want to fail to say that the good weather came yesterday, the day of the presentation of Holy Mary. Long live our Mother! God only knows how much you prayed on my behalf! I've often thought about it. Even my aunt, the nun, and the other nuns promised to help me with their prayers. God has heard them. Speaking of my aunt, the nun, I often thought about what the good Sister

Maria Luisa said to me, and it made me laugh even the day we had the storm: "When you are at sea," said Sister Maria Luisa, "and the weather is bad, stop [and get off], you know." Today I said to myself that one should do what Sister Maria Luisa said, and get off at some hotel some hundreds of miles away. . . .

Sunday, November 23, 9:00 A.M.

Today the sea is not just calm, it's perfectly flat. It's a delight: the skies are clear and the water hardly moves; everyone is on deck taking in this delight. I came down for a moment to write to you about it, and to offer thanks to God. What a beautiful day! This morning a public Holy Mass was held. All of the Catholics were present, and many Protestants, too.

Sunday November 23, 11:30 A.M.

Land, Land! Blessed be the Lord. At this moment we see land again for the first time since Ireland. It is a long island close to New York, and called, in fact, *Long Island*. Just now the captain has announced that there are only seventy miles to go. Maybe we will arrive before dark and even be able to disembark this very evening. This morning three large whales came dancing toward us as if to welcome us. If you had seen them; they were like three ships in a storm; that's how big they were. *Benedicite cete et omnia quae moventur in aquis Domino* [Bless the Lord, you whales and all that move in the sea]. Today is a day of great happiness for all. The journey has been somewhat difficult, but today everything is forgotten, and these past two days have been a gift of Providence.

Sunday 23 – 7:00 P.M.

At 6:30 precisely we anchored in Sandy Hook harbor where all the ships stop to allow for a medical inspection before proceeding for

New York, which is only a few miles away.[2] But it is too late for the inspection so we will have to spend the night here in this port. Tomorrow morning, after the health commission arrives and conducts its inspection, we will be able, with the help of God, to put foot on land in New York.

Today it was a magnificent day; the sea was like a mirror. In brief, this good ending makes us forget the past, and we are all very happy. Blessed be God.

Monday 24 – 9:00 A.M.

We have had our medical inspection, but we can't leave for New York yet because of a very thick fog which has reduced visibility to zero. We will have to wait. It's a bit annoying to be so close to our destination and still not be able to reach it. We have to be patient as it's but a slight inconvenience. I am still hoping that our patron Saint will make it possible for me to go thank him in our Church in New York.

Monday 24, 12:00 A.M.

At half past eleven the fog finally started to lift and now we are headed for New York where, God willing, we will arrive in an hour.

New York
Monday 24, 3:00 P.M.

Here we are, not only on land, but also among our Fathers and brothers of this beautiful College of St. Francis. May the Lord be thanked. I don't have to tell you how happy these good Fathers were to see us, and how warmly they welcomed us. We will stay here for a few days. At the customs we were lucky enough to go through the only catholic employee to be found there. When, by our address, he saw who we were, he whispered: "Did you have a good trip?" and didn't even open our suitcases. This freed us of many delays and we were able to come right away to our house where we later found out that that employee was one of our former students.

I think this letter will leave tomorrow (25), because Europe-bound leaves not every day, but two or three times a week. I am hoping it won't be long before it will arrive to reassure you. . . .

As you can see the Lord has protected us. Our journey was somewhat trying, but everyone here says that to have traveled three thousand miles in only ten days in this season is extraordinary. Soon after we arrived at the port something happened that quite surprised us. We had boarded some sort of coach to go to the College, and the coach, along with many others in front and behind, entered a sort of tunnel built of wood. There the horses stopped in the tunnel. We thought that there might be some obstruction and that we might have to wait. We stayed in the coach wondering what the delay was about. After six or seven minutes we heard a bell ring twice and soon we were in the open air again. What had happened? All the carriages coming from the port board a ferry, where there are stable-like structures. The steamship, then ferries everything across the river where the city is located. Someone who doesn't know this, doesn't realize what is happening.

Tuesday November 25 — St. Catherine's Day

Today, during the Holy Mass, I thought about auntie and Mrs. Ricci. I also prayed for all of you. For the love and glory of God we are now separated from one another by an entire Ocean, but God repays us for what we do for him. When I set foot in this country, I felt a great consolation knowing that I am closer to my dear Natives to whom God has called me. This morning, the first Mass I said in America, I offered it especially for the well-being of that Mission. How good and merciful the Lord is!

I end this letter with a thousand warm greetings to all of you. Without naming each of you, I'd want you to believe I think of you, and of the love for me that you have shown in so many ways. The

Chartreuse and the *Acqua della scala*, given to me by my aunts, were of great help to me on the ship on bad days.³ Thank you ever so much.

I embrace you with my heart, and I leave you in the holy hearts of Jesus and Mary. Goodbye.

Your most affectionate

Philip, Apostolic Missionary.

[7]

Journey from New York to St. Louis

St. Louis, Missouri, December 10, 1873

P. C.

Dearest Parents and relatives,

I wrote you twice from New York. Now I write this hurriedly to let you know that I won't be spending the winter in St. Louis, and that I will continue right away my trip to the Mission. The Father Superior left for me a letter in which he assigns me to the Residence of St. Mary's among the Flathead tribe, and tells me that I may go there immediately. From here the trip will be different from the one I told you Father Guidi took, also because this is a different season. I will not go via the River, but by rail for three or four days and then I will take what they call the *stage* for a few more days. There isn't a lot of snow yet, and we can travel comfortably to the end of the trip. The Father Superior recommended that we provide ourselves with plenty of furs, blankets, and the like. The Fathers here took me to a St. Louis store and dressed me like a bear. All you can see are my eyes and my mouth. The rest is fur from all kinds of animals. If I could send you a picture, you would see a real wild animal. I believe that if we were to encounter a true one, he would jump on our back solely for the satisfaction of seeing that even we have adopted their fashion. We will dress so only when we are in the mountains, otherwise, if they saw us dressed like this in the city, I think they would immediately put us in a zoo, but we have better things to do than just stay in a cage and nourish the curiosity of idle people.

I received a letter here from Father Guidi who is excited as you can imagine about my arrival. He is staying at Fort Colville, which is quite far from St. Mary's, so we probably won't see each other for quite some time because everyone remains obediently at his assigned post, and cultivates that part of the vineyard that God has assigned him.[1]

I received another letter today that Father Guidi had sent to Tronchiennes and the Tronchiennes fathers forwarded to me here. This letter was written in October, and because Father Guidi already knew of my desire to come among these dear Natives it pleases me to read that: "The Indians pray that my [Rappagliosi's] wish be fulfilled and they hope to see me [Rappagliosi] soon among them."

Now I'll tell you something about my trip from New York to St. Louis. I left New York the evening of November 28th and I arrived the next morning at our College in Baltimore.[2] From there I went to see our College at Woodstock which was only one hour away by train.[3] Many of them were Italians and old friends of mine. It was a big party. They absolutely insisted on keeping me there for three days; I don't know how I managed to get away. After thirty hours on the train I arrived at Cincinnati where I stayed at our residence for only a few hours; then I continued to St. Louis without problems, arriving there the following evening. In any case we covered the 1,064 miles from New York to St. Louis in the long journey from Rome to here without any trouble, except the cup of coffee Father O'Flinn sent flying out of my hand when he turned to order a roll to dip into it.

Let's talk now about something else concerning the land journey. I would like to describe the American train cars to you, but as I am in a hurry, it will be difficult to tell you everything. To have an idea you should imagine entering so many large rooms, each twice as big as our European cars, and each with doors at both ends so that one can walk from car to car without getting off the train. Each car has two stoves, a small bathroom, drinking water, and water for washing. One can move about the car as one pleases, as there is an aisle in the middle and seats on the sides. The sleeping cars are fancier and more comfortable. Each berth has a lamp, a mirror, and a couch which turns, as if by magic, into a bed for the night. I won't be able to describe this for you, but I can tell you that in one moment where you were sitting, you now have a bed as large as a single bed one finds in a house. The uniformed attendant in each car makes the bed and draws a magnificent curtain around each bed; so that each person had a sort of private room of his own. Having read in Father Guidi's letter an account of all of this, I already knew what to expect. Yet the experience exceeded my expectations and I was left mouth agape like the country bumpkin peasant who comes to Rome for the first time. No one may smoke in the car, but, there is a smoking room for those who wish to smoke. And then the speed of American trains is really extraordinary, as you have heard, and he who goes at breakneck speed may actually break his neck.

All comforts, my dear ones, are over for me, this has been the last greeting progress has sent me. In truth, I hardly answered that greeting, first of all because progress, the seed of which God himself planted in humans, through human fault often makes humans forget Him from whom all things begin and to whom all things return; and second, because the simplicity of the poor people among whom I am about to go, has a special enchantment. Even the Latin poet turned his eyes away from the palaces of the Caesars [or the emperors or the rich], and looked toward fields and farmers saying: *oh fortunati sua si bona norint* [lucky are those who know how good they have it].

This said, I don't mean to speak ill of the cars that have taken me so fast and so well. God forbid! All I am saying is . . . I don't need to explain, I'm sure you understand.

I want you to understand one more thing, and I'll be done. In the place where I am going there are no trains, and everything moves slowly. And when there is a lot of snow, things don't just move slowly, they don't move at all. What am I trying to say? I mean that you shouldn't be surprised if my letters, especially in winter, reach you quite late, if at all.

Don't worry, if my letters get stuck in the snow, my dear Indians will see to it that their writer stays close to a fire. I just want you to start thinking that you shouldn't worry. All this follows the offer that I and you have made to God, so we shouldn't wonder, but find comfort in the Lord who will take account of everything for us.

Goodbye, Goodbye. I always pray for you. Greetings and greetings to all. . . .

Yours,

Philip S.J., Apostolic Missionary.

[8]
Journey to and Arrival at the Rocky Mountains

Helena, December 26, 1873

P. C.

Dearest Parents and relatives.

I have already told you why I did not stay in St. Louis. The morning of the eleventh of December we continued on our journey to Helena, Montana, where, with the help of the Lord, we arrived safely the evening of the twenty-first. More than two thousand miles stretch from St. Louis to Helena. A great part of the trip we traveled by rail, sleeping three nights in the cars in the manner that I described in my last letter. At Corinne we got off the train and began traveling in quite a different way.[1] – The first day on a sled drawn by two horses across a long snow-covered valley. This means of travel has but the inconvenience that one has to ride in the open, bundled up in furs and blankets. But as for the rest, the sled moves along easily across the surface of frozen snow, and shakes the riders much less than the *stage*. We traveled this way from six in the morning until seven in the evening. We spent the night in a hotel where we had a good bed and enjoyed a sound sleep. But it wasn't to be so the nights that followed. The next, after a few hours of travel by sled, we boarded a coach or *stage*, as they call them here. There wasn't as much snow here as there had been, thus we traveled by wheeled carriage. These so-called *stages* resemble our diligences, but covered with canvas, old and torn like the rest, in short a thing for the mountains.[2] The 482 miles from Corinne to Helena are traveled by sled or stage, depending on how deep the snow is.

Since the roads are nearly always rough and steep they change horses at least every two hours; and every fifty or sixty miles they change carriage and driver. Note that we travel night and day without interruption. . . .

The changing of stagecoaches is a bit of an inconvenience for the passengers, because each day [each time] the bags have to be unloaded and loaded, but that makes for greater travel safety; because the stage that you have at a given point returns to the place where it had picked you up, the drivers and the horses always travel the same fifty miles, and get to know the road well. The chance of getting lost in those snowy plains, or of falling off a cliff is much lessened. We did the entire trip to Helena by sled or by stage, six days and four nights continuously, sleeping only on two occasions on the ground, wrapped in blankets next to a big fire. You probably think that we suffered a great deal, but it wasn't nearly as bad as we had thought. In the end all we suffered was a little fatigue, due to the continuous motion and the loss of sleep, but this is easily cured as soon as one finds a place to lie down and sleep, and here in Helena, at the residence of the Fathers, we have had much help and rest. If it hadn't been for the holy feast [Christmas] we would have continued the bit of journey that remains. As you can see, everything has gone well and the Lord has protected us in a special way. We could count on his help because such a trip in the middle of winter, was an exercise in obedience, and the Lord doesn't abandon anyone who executes his will in everything. One night in particular we had evidence of his protection.

That night we were traveling on a wagon lying as best we could on sacks of mail and baggage. With every bump and sway we had to hold onto the sacks [so as] not to roll off into the snow, or worse, under the horses' hooves. The night was quite dark and we were white with snow from head to foot. And then the driver, who was half asleep, shook himself awake and started looking in every direction. He then stopped the horses and got off without a word. It didn't take us long to realize that we had strayed off the road because of the snow. We were in the middle of an immense plain, far from any houses, and did not know where. The driver started to walk trying to find tracks. Finally, as God willed, he came back to us, and after wandering about for some time, we found the road again. We arrived at the first horse station after seventeen miles at around midnight. There the driver rearranged the sacks and baggage so that we could sit and proceed less uncomfortably until nine in the morning. That poor fellow was really tired, and I had to shake him several times to keep him from straying off the road again: when I noticed the horses pounding on the snow, right then I elbowed the driver, and he would pull the horses. That was the first test, so to speak, of our apostolate, and thanks to God, we made it okay, with determination and cheer, and furthermore, in good health. Many times we joined Brother Melchers in saying: "How many stay inside close to the fireplace and yet have coughs! A journey to the Rocky Mountains in the month of December, is the real remedy, that delivers from all ills confirmed by forty years of success!"

Arrived at Helena, we are happy to be among our brothers.[3] Helena is a small city of Whitemen (around three thousand) and is the largest city of Whites in the Montana Territory. What has attracted them here are gold and silver mines. We have a small residence here consisting of two Fathers and a brother, and we try, as much as possible, to keep these people, who have come to dig earthly riches, from losing the heavenly ones. Last night at midnight our little Church was full of people, and this was no small pleasure.

Monday, December 29th, we will leave for St. Mary's where, finally, we will be among our dear Natives. This journey will be easier because we travel only by day. Besides, St. Mary's is only 153 miles from Helena, which now seems to us a short walk. In two or three days I will be able to sing a nice Te Deum, more than two months after I left Rome.[4]

I hope you get this letter by St. Agnes's day, so that it can give Mama a reason to celebrate. I wish you all a Happy New Year. God has given me the wonderful gift of starting the new year at the Mission. May his mercy always be blessed!!! . . . Goodbye.

I embrace all of you with all my heart. Rest assured, I pray for all of you.

Your most affectionate son
Philip S.J., Apostolic Missionary.

[9]

First News from the Missions

St. Mary's Mission January 6, 1874
Epiphany of the Lord.

P. C.

Dearest Parents,

I don't know if you've received all my letters. You have probably written some too, but since I have been constantly on the road, your letters may have been following me, but haven't yet caught up with me. I have finally arrived two months and ten days after leaving Rome.[1] On January 3rd I set foot at our Residence at St. Mary's among the Flathead tribe. I arrived in good health and grateful to the Lord for having helped and protected us. For now, I can't tell you much about this mission. I will wait to write letters full of news until I am better acquainted with things here. Today I will be satisfied with telling you some of my first impressions. The Indians had already been told by Father D'Aste that I would be arriving. As soon as they saw me they came to greet me. They shook my hand and said *gest sgalgalt* (good day) and *lemlemt lemlent* (I am glad). I will always remember that wonderful moment. I was impressed most by the good old wife of the old tribal chief: she held both of my hands and seemed so heartened that I was moved to see such faith and warmth.[2] This is all the result of the hard work of the Fathers that have preceded me. This morning, Epiphany day, I saw (just as Father Guidi had written) the mothers step up to receive Communion with their little children tied behind their back. In church they recite their prayers out loud and they sing. Their singing amounts to bringing forth all of the voice they have in their bodies, and the result of this is a harmony that you can imagine. Yet they love music and when they hear the Fathers sing they are as in ecstasy.

Yesterday I went to visit one of their lodges. It is a cone-shaped hut made of buffalo hides with a hole at the top to let the smoke out.[3] The fire is in the middle, and around it are strewn more skins on which they sit during the day and sleep at night. For now I am satisfied to ask them: *suet askuest* (what is your name)? The first Indian woman I met is called *Agnese* and the chief of the tribe is called *Carlo*: what do you say of this coincidence?[4] I also found out that one of the boys is called *Pilip* – Philip – The Indians don't have the letter *f*, and replace it with the letter *p* in the baptismal names. Yesterday an Indian who came to see me said to the other Father: "You are an old *blackrobe*, this one is a *new blackrobe*." He meant, you are old and he is young.

I am busy studying their language, I have as many teachers as I want. With the help of God, I hope to get by in it. These good Indians help me patiently; I think I too have patience. Many things can be accomplished with this fine virtue.

If I don't receive any news from you soon, I will have to resign myself because I know that in winter letters arrive with great difficulty here, so far and with so much snow. You too, must feel the same way if my letters don't arrive or if they arrive late. If everything goes well it takes a month from here to Rome, the Fathers tell me. In any case, we have made this sacrifice to God, so now we accept the consequences for his glory and for the salvation of the souls. This is a small matter if one considers what we owe God. Isn't it true?

Not to delay this letter further today, I will take advantage of the mail pick-up. Hearty greetings to all. I often think of the days we have spent together! We are not as far apart from each other as one might think, for God bands us together (after this sacrifice made for his love) with ties of greater and purer affection. Goodbye. I leave you in the holy hearts of Jesus and Mary. . . .

Say hello to all of my dear Fathers and brothers everywhere.

All yours,

Philip, Apostolic Missionary, S.J.

10

Customs of the Indians

Stevensville, February 13, 1874.

P. C.

Dearest Parents and relatives,

The day before yesterday I received with the greatest consolation *your first letter* since I left Europe! The two letters which succeeded in finding me among my Indians, were the one of December 13 from Francesco, Enrico, Paolo, and Mother. In the one of the thirteenth there was the icon of Saint Raffaele who, as you see, accompanied the letter well. Thus God be praised that I have good news from all of you and that I see you happy and comforted. I am also glad to hear that my letters from New York and the previous ones reached you. I hope this will also be the case for the others where I described the rest of my trip from Baltimore, St. Louis, Helena and finally from this Mission of Saint Mary. Of your letters, as I said, only these two arrived. Both have a postage of fifty-five centesimi on them, but fifty would have been sufficient, equivalent to ten cents in American money as you can see from my letters.

Now I answer each letter separately; starting with Father and Mother's.

I thank Father a lot for the Masses that he had that holy prelate say for me. God surely protected me in a special way. Mother asks me at first if I am in good health. The answer is unequivocal. I am in excellent health and better than when you last saw me in Rome, so that it seems that we can be satisfied. Just today when the Father Superior saw me, he said: "Here he is, fresh as a rose, Father Philip."

I hear with pleasure that you always say the three little prayers I asked you to say. This way you contribute to the good I do here, and you, too, are apostles to these dear souls. Many thanks also to my aunts for their prayers. As to the woolen mittens, be assured Mother, that I am prepared for the cold here better than you can imagine.

The methods that are used here to protect oneself from the cold, and the very warm and comfortable hides that we have, are not known in Europe. In other words, you see the cold but you don't feel it, and the things I brought from Europe to stay warm, I think I will wear them in springtime! I already wrote to you that in St. Louis we had to dress like two bears. So much for the woolen mittens. As for beards, the Fathers here don't wear them, because the Indians not only don't let it grow but don't even have the roots! It's their custom to pluck out their whiskers one by one as soon as they appear on their chins. That's why you can see young men wearing some kind of tweezers on their chests to pluck out whatever whisker grows. Only their head hair is allowed to grow at will, and they wear it long and black, even the old ones, and when they ride on horseback it flows majestically in the wind on their shoulders. And so I have satisfied Mother's questions. . . .

It reassured me to learn of your Christian feelings about my leaving for this mission. That is how God can take everything to its completion.

A few days ago I was invited to see our other mission, Saint Ignatius among the Kalispels. There is a nice wooden church, the best in the whole mission. It has three naves and is completely whitewashed without base paint. On my way back, going through Missoula, I heard that two Indian women had come the day before, looking for a Blackrobe to baptize a girl. Luckily they were told about my trip and they turned around on their horses. They named her Marianna, and this is my first-born in Jesus Christ here in the mountains.[1]

When I came back to Saint Mary's I was happy to see my Indians come to shake my hand and greet me warmly with their greeting, *gest sgalgat* — Pilip —good day Philip. So far it seems that the name Pilip or Philip is the one that will stay with me. It's easy for them to remember and they don't have to use other names. If it will be so, my good patron Saint Philip will not be forgotten.

In the evening I say prayers with them in Church, and ask them the questions of the Catechism. If you feel like making the sign of the cross in the Flathead language, that's what you would say: *Lkuests Leu u skusse a st spgpagt komi ezgeil*. . . .

I embrace and greet you all warmly. Keep well and joyful in our Lord who comforts copiously those who sacrifice themselves for his love; and pray to him that he helps me with his grace, so that I may search in everything only his glory and the execution of his lovable divine will! Goodbye. Goodbye.

Yours forever

Philip S.J., Apostolic Missionary.

[11]

First Good Deeds

Stevensville, March 3, 1874

P. C.

Dearest Parents and all my relatives,

First of all a happy and holy Easter from your affectionate Philip. I have to take aim well in advance if I want my letter to arrive in time for Easter. So sing joyful *alleluia* to our Lord, also because your Philip is so well and happy among those dear Indians, so that the Lord is really to be blessed. As I think I wrote in my last letter for the moment the task at hand is to learn two languages at the same time, English and the Indian Kalispel. The latter is indeed different from any other European language but with the help of God, who has called me, I think I will soon be able to say something. Maybe I will give my first little sermon for the feast of Saint Joseph.[1] In the meantime I practice saying my prayers with the Natives morning and evening and I do the Catechism twice a day, being satisfied at the moment with the questions and answers as they stand in the book handwritten and painstakingly compiled by the first Fathers to arrive here. I cannot tell you with how much solace in my soul I spend time with these poor people, so simple and good, and so eager to learn about the things of God and of the soul. Every Indian is a friend and brother to me, because God has put them in my charge with all his goodness and mercy, saying to me: "Leave your parents and friends and I will give you as many friends and brothers in those abandoned souls that I have redeemed." This little tribe of the Flatheads is a small but chosen portion of Jesus Christ's flock. There are just over four hundred of them, but they are devoted to religion and pious practices.

We get good and reassuring news from the larger tribes as well. In sum the Indians receive and safeguard the treasure of faith, and on judgment day they will put to shame many White people.

Now a large part of the tribe hunts buffalo the whole winter, but today we got the first news of their return. At Easter they will all be here and this is a great celebration for the whole camp. They always quit the hunt in time to be in Church and to confess and receive communion on that solemn occasion. We have heard that this year, thank God, the Flatheads had run-ins neither with the Crows nor with the Blackfeet, both enemy tribes.[2] The Blackfeet Indians are very numerous: more than eleven thousand.

When a group of them hunting runs into an enemy tribe, they try to take and steal their horses, and in consequence there are often injuries and deaths on both sides.

Buffalo hunting is far away, about three hundred miles at least, so they stay for long periods without there being news of them; it's only toward the end of the hunt that some leave the camp ahead of the rest and bring news to those who had stayed behind. So today two Pend d'Oreilles on horseback arrived here and the whole camp was abuzz with the good news before and after the Mass.

The Pend d'Oreilles are friends of the Flatheads; as are the Nez Perces, the Snakes and other tribes.[3] So often they find themselves hunting together.

The Nez Perces number about six thousand and they, too, show good disposition toward the things of God. They speak a different language: but Indians of all tribes share a common language with which they communicate: that is to say the sign language in which they can express themselves beyond belief. Usually the whole Family goes hunting, men, women, youngsters: they carry on one horse the poles and the Buffalo hides for their tents, and they ride the others, and off they go; the house is so nice that it can be transported anywhere. It's incredible how the Indians can ride on horseback; all their tack equipment is a rope at the horse's neck, and men, women, and children just go as though one with the horses. In addition, often a horse carries several people. I've often seen a mother and four children get on a horse and run off: if one of the kids is too small, they put him in some kind of sack that hangs on one side of the horse and bounces at the horse's will: one must say that these jarrings settle the children's bones, because when they arrive I've seen them well and calm as if they had been in a cradle. But enough for today about our dear Natives. – Now some news about some fellow missionaries whom you know or about whom I have written before.

Brother Melchers is here in Saint Mary's and he too is fine and happy. Father Guidi, who came here a bit less than a year before me, has written to me already two or three times from Colville where he is situated and he is doing well. Colville is at a ten or twelve days' distance from here: from this you can imagine how long and wide our field is, and yet this is only a little corner of America and of the United States. When I went to visit the other Mission at Saint Ignatius, two days away from here, I happened to go with another Father to visit a sick man. His place was far from Saint Ignatius because he had gone Deer hunting with his Family. The two of us went and we traveled on horseback without seeing anything but wide plains and high mountains, and without meeting anything but two wolves who stopped to watch us from a distance. The Father said to me: look there, and went ahead. I had never been so close to such animals, unless they were caged. I should note that these wolves here will hardly attack you, if you don't attack them. They are prairie wolves: most vicious is the grizzly bear that lives in the mountains: but even then there is special protection from God. None of the Fathers who have lived here for many years has been attacked so far, although more than one of them has run across these creatures.

I wrote this as it came to mind but later I hope to send to Europe some letters that might be read with pleasure and interest, and even published, so that these Missions, for the glory of God, may become known and loved. . . .

All yours
Philip, Missionary, S.J.

[12]

Piousness of the Catholic Indians at Easter

Stevensville, April 11, 1874

P. C.

Dearest Parents and relatives,

Almost all the Indians have come back from the buffalo hunt. Only ten lodges or families did not arrive in time for Easter, because with so much snow covering the country, their horses had suffered from hunger. But yesterday I heard that these families are closer and will soon arrive, and will go to confession like all the others. Oh, how nice the Easter holiday is among our Natives. When I say nice holiday, you shouldn't think a nice setup, many lights and what have you. In this regard we are very poor, but our poor wooden Church is adorned by the pious congregation of the Indians, by their faith and their prayers. On Maundy Thursday family by family came to visit the pitiable Sepulcher and they prayed and sang. Of course their songs are the songs of Indians: it's not strictly speaking music: nevertheless, since the Fathers worked hard to teach them even singing, one can recognize amidst great shrieking this or that tune, this or that aria, but altered and counterfeited as they please. Nevertheless God is certainly fully satisfied with that. Then on Good Friday they came to the adoration of the Cross: one after the other approached the Cross laid out on a blanket on the floor to kiss it. In the evening they came to the sermon about the passion of Our Lord and they listened with feelings of faith and piety. The Indian who weeps so rarely is nevertheless moved to tears when he hears about the suffering of Our Lord. That very Good Friday I saw one leave the Church red-eyed and teary. At first I thought he was not well because, as I said, it's extremely rare to see a Native cry, and without thought I asked him, what happened to your eyes? Are you not well? And he answered: "Oh, blackrobe, I am not sick, but I cried in Church today because Our Lord died." On Easter Sunday a great number came to receive communion. I don't think there is one Indian who refuses to come to these highest sacraments especially during these more important feasts. The Church was full and some stood outside the door. While the Father was dressing for the Mass, one of the chiefs stood up and addressed the others in the following way: (I give you here his whole little speech in its entirety, and it's just as he said it, because I called him to my room, made him repeat it, and I wrote it down, and now I translate it verbatim into Italian for you.) "Men and women, you all went to confession and you all want to go to communion now. Will you perhaps again take up sins afterward? If you go to communion when you intend to sin again, that is a great sin, if you confessed when you intend to sin again, that's a great sin. I am finished."[1] Then High Mass began. The Indians have learned (who would have believed it?) to sing the *Gloria*, the *Credo*, and all the rest and they sing it firmly: at least that was the intent of the Father who first taught them.[2] The same with the *Regina coeli* during Easter time.[3] In sum, much simplification, but much faith and piety. Of course that day they were all dressed up, that is those who had one had wrapped themselves in a new wool blanket, or else in the hide of a buffalo killed in the last hunt. Then red paint on their faces, only on the forehead, or only on the cheeks, or only on the chins, or all over the face, ears, and neck according to one's taste; and seashells, glass beads, shards, and brass or iron wire twisted around their braids, and necklaces of all colors and mirrors and Crucifixes and medals dangling on their chests, and all the rest which I will describe at greater leisure some other time. In other words carnival wear for us, but for them the latest fashion.

This week I went to visit a few Indian huts either along the river or at the foot of the mountain, scattered at a distance of two or three miles from each other. Note, that there are only a few among the Natives who have frame houses, because they live wherever there is room to set up a few poles in a circle, tie them together at the top, and cover them with buffalo skins. This is their movable home. Nevertheless there are a few who have started to farm the land, and these have a fixed house, that is to say, a fixed one-room log structure. So I went to see them and to hang up in their houses a few nice icons of the Heart of Jesus and of Mary. I assure you that I returned home very happy that evening. They had received me with as much welcome as Indians can give. The little Indians were the first ones to see the Blackrobe approaching, and I saw them leave their games and go inside to tell the family, "Pilip, good day, Pilip." While I was inside someone would hold my horse or tie it to a tree, and not let me do it myself. Right away we talked, I asked if they had gone to confession, if they love Jesus and Mary, and if they shun sin; there is no need to wait for the right opportunity to talk about these things. The opportunity is always there, and you just have to talk to be understood.

Pilip (one said to me), a mile from here there is a girl who is not well and couldn't go to Church; go take her confession. In fact I found that poor girl and she did her confession. There I also found a blind old woman who also wanted to confess because she couldn't come to Church, not only because it's far away, but also because those houses are across the river which one has to cross on horseback. I led her to a tree, because the sick girl couldn't leave the one-room dwelling, and there I confessed the blind woman who stood up and thanked me profusely, shaking my hand as if I had given her back her eyesight. That's the faith of the Indians. In another house I said to a cripple, "How unfortunate you are, poor Michael," and he said, "Yes, indeed, but I shall not be unfortunate in Heaven." – Good lesson by a Catholic Indian.[4]

I don't have to tell you how glad they were to receive those pictures. In general the Indians appreciate and love medals, Crucifixes, and rosaries because they are easier to keep, but those who have houses love the icons because they can hang them. They keep all these things like treasures. While I was in one house hanging those pictures an old woman took out a package and started to unwrap it: out came some rolled papers. What was it? A very old picture in pieces, as yellow as the wax of the Holy Week. These fragments of picture were wrapped around a stick of wood and the old woman said: "See, thirty snows ago (that is to say, thirty winters, or thirty years ago) Father DeSmet gave this to me! and then she rolled everything up again and wrapped it like a treasure. . . .

I embrace you with all my heart.

All yours

Philip S.J., Apostolic Missionary.

[13]

Way of Life among the Indians and Good Deeds

Stevensville, May 5, 1874

P. C.

Dearest Parents and all relatives,

The thirtieth of April I received your dear letter of March 23. . . .

Dad asked me about the Baby Jesus. From my other letters you probably already know that it arrived in pieces. Now it's in the care of the Nuns of Missoula and we will see what becomes of it.[1]

Now let's turn to our beverages. Our beverage is very simple, excellent and it's always available. You already understand that I am speaking of fresh water which is really good in this region, and the trevi's water is no match.[2] For the Mass we get a little bit of wine from California; and since the purchase and the shipping are so terribly expensive, we order only what we need, we use it only for the consecration during the Mass; for the two ablutions that follow, we have the permission to use just water; so the wine for the Mass lasts much longer.[3] At meals one can have *Coffee* or *tea* if one wants to – We can get these two beverages more easily from the Whites who live nearby, they cost less and the Indians, too, often go sell deer and buffalo skins in order to get coffee, tea, and sugar from the whites. In almost the whole of North America this is the usual beverage for lunch and dinner: but many don't like hot drinks with their meals and therefore we turn to fresh and limpid water, which is a pleasure. As for food, we are much better off then I thought we would be; we have different kinds of meat, but mostly pork and beef. We have cows which give us good milk, and hens which give us eggs when they are young, and broth when they are old. Then potatoes and carrots, much better than those from Belgium which are already big and good. We have good wheat, good flour, and good bread, made by a brother. In short, I came here prepared for the worst, and so this now seems a delight. And in fact I am in very good health and feel very strong. If God helps me I want to do some good to this good tribe, as well as to the other one, which is not yet good because not converted:

I am talking about other tribes nearby. I forgot to tell you that when it comes to fish we are really the first lords of the world here. I have not seen such good and tasty fish anywhere else. The Indians often bring us some: if you saw how beautiful! You will never find the like in the fish-market. When you cross the river on horseback you can see them jump, as if to say: take me, take me. – The boys stand there with a hook and they eat them for lunch and for dinner. They come and ask us for fishhooks: we have obtained a good supply, a fishhook is a big present for the Indians.

The other day a boy said to me: "Give me a fishhook, blackrobe:" then in the evening he came back with a magnificent fish which we weighed, just out of curiosity. It was over seven pounds. And how did you manage to catch it with a hook, I asked him? He answered with a laugh that meant: The way we and others like us do it. . . .

Dad would like a new photo of me. But it's too soon, and you have one taken a few months ago: how different do you think I would be? And there is another reason why I won't send you one, there are no photographers around here. That's a good reason, I think. Maybe later we'll see if I can't let you have at least a drawing of my beloved Indians, of their true friend Pilip, and of our little wooden Church, etc. etc.

That's all as an answer to the letter of March 23. Now the news from here, but first the one who will read this letter to the others should take a break and have a drink to our health. For today, I'll rest my pen too. Until tomorrow.

May 6, 1874

P. C.

I continue my letter of yesterday, and first let me tell you that I am really happy because I am starting to speak the language of the Flatheads a little. Several times a week I go on my rounds on horseback to see them. I teach the Catechism with the youngsters who all know me and congregate by me. In Church, too, I do Catechism every day, morning and evening. With the Indians you can't get tired of repeating the same thing a thousand times. The Father Superior has already written to me that by July I should be ready to accompany him to the tribe of the Kalispels who also speak the same language. They are already baptized, but we go to give them a little mission, as we have done before with other tribes. Then if the Lord helps me I want to learn some other language.

There are many Native tribes and their languages are quite different. One is not related to the other. See, for example, how the Flatheads say "Jesus, Joseph, and Mary, may my soul expire in peace with you [may I die in peace]":

They say:

Jesus Mary Joseph die with you in peace
Jesu, Mali, Zose, ilkamkemt, lanui ikaespopeulsem
my soul.
isingapeus.

The Kootenais instead say:

Jesus Mary Joseph die with you
Jesu Mali, Zosep machutsuan gamni ninkonissemil
in peace   my soul
kakannuckuaskommik kutuklululak.

The latter have some very long words. They call the priesthood *Jakaokualetiamkikam kokokolkatuumlat.*

Of course these are compound words and the one just cited, literally translated, doesn't mean Priesthood, but the *office of one who wears the black robe.*

The other day four Indians from the Nez Perce tribe came here, and they speak a third language which is as related to the others as Turkish is to Italian.[4] They had come to be baptized. They were accompanied by another Nez Perce who is already baptized, knows the Catechism well, and also speaks the language of the Flatheads. With his help I now try to instruct the others. They'll come back tonight. In the meantime two Nez Perce women, Catholics, came running here. Oh, if you had seen their fervor: how they were trying

to teach the others themselves! My room was full of Indians kneeling in front of an icon of Jesus on the cross and Holy Mary. Even
those not baptized knelt down. I was moved to tears. I hope in two or
three weeks they will be well instructed, and on their way to eternal
salvation. In sum, we should learn at least six or seven Indian languages if we want to help everybody. With the help of God we will
do as much as we can. Of course the good disposition of those Indians is of great encouragement to the Missionary, and you mustn't
stop praying for me.

Last Saturday I was called to assist a dying woman; she was on
the floor lying on a buffalo skin.[5] The place was full of Indians who
had come to pray. I felt real consolation seeing how the sick woman,
until her last, gathering whatever strength she still had, lifted her
arm and her hand touched her forehead, her chest, and her shoulders. [She crossed herself.] She was not able to speak anymore, but she
did what she could, and with such faith that I stayed there watching her with admiration. Would you believe it? She died making the
Christians' sign: her hand fell on her chest, and she was with our
Lord just as I was giving her the last absolution.[6] What do you think
about that? Don't you bless our Lord? Aren't you happy about what
you have done? For my part, I think that just one such single act is a
great reward, and I'm sure you feel the same.

You should have heard the prayers that the Indians were saying.
One of the women said: "God, my Lord, have mercy on this dying
woman. She is suffering now but soon she will be rejoicing with you,
because she has confessed her sins. God, my Lord, have mercy on her;
Mary, Mother of God, have mercy on her." She was silent for a moment, then she added: "Soon we might by lying like this, too, called
by God. Lord, have mercy on us." – Then she recited the act of contrition, and the others joined in, word after word. What a beautiful
scene!

I thought that the Fathers had taught them these prayers, to be
recited in such circumstances, and that that was the custom. Then I
learned, however, that it wasn't so, and that this Indian woman was
just following her heart. One should know what these Indians were

like forty years earlier to understand the sublimity of that prayer, and all the beauty of their faith.

I've done quite a few baptisms. May 1, the day of Saint Philip and Saint James, I gave one the name of Philip (Pilip).[7] Usually they themselves propose names and it's better to give them the choice. Among these good Indians, I have found almost all the names you have.

(I interrupt again because the Nez Perces have come back to be instructed. We will continue later.)

Here I am again for you. I don't want to miss telling you about a custom that prevails among the Natives here, that is to give a feast for the whole tribe two or three days after one of their relatives has died.[8] Two or three oxen are killed according to one's means, and on that day everybody is invited. I don't know where this custom comes from, but I think that, while it was in use before the arrival of the Fathers, now it has taken on an almost religious character, I would say, the way it is practiced. A day when one of these Indian feasts was taking place, two or three of the tribe came to me and said: "Blackrobe, you, too, come and eat with us.["] I took advantage of the opportunity and the invitation to see how things were done. I remained very satisfied with it all. Imagine two or three lodges joined in the shape of a big tent or cabin formed by hide. The men were sitting on the ground in a circle under the tent and behind them were the boys. Behind were the women and the girls in a circle, and finally the dogs which formed a third circle far back, and they, too, were waiting for something, only a little hungrier than their masters. When I arrived the chief had me sit down on a buffalo hide. They were all in silence and the chief said: Come Blackrobe and see all your children. As customary the silence wasn't broken by any other voice: two or three stepped into the middle to cut into pieces the quarters of the ox which were already more or less cooked. During this ceremony which lasted a long time, two or three of the chiefs made their speeches. They eulogized the deceased. Then some of them took their blankets off their backs and, to honor me, spread them in front of me. They did the same with the chiefs. Then they took the pieces of meat and put them in little piles on the blankets. When I saw that everything was ready and all that was left was to reach for the food and eat, I said: Children, let us make the sign of the cross and pray. You shouldn't think that if I hadn't said anything the Indians wouldn't have done so. It doesn't happen that the Indians start to eat without saying a prayer. Then they laid hands on their work, still in silence. Only the chiefs could talk, standing up to make their speeches. For me it was a real pleasure to listen to them, they were saying beautiful things, and you know, they always do that, and they were not things said because I was there. One said: "Men and women, we grieve when someone dies, but find consolation thinking of Heaven, where we will all be called."

And another chief said, even more eloquently: "My people, you are now feasting because Susanna has died, but you don't know when the others will feast for you. Perhaps in a few days another ox will be butchered for the death of one of us. Maybe we will die at home, maybe hunting: we don't know. So forsake sin and prepare yourselves." Then at the end they gave the condolences to the relatives of the deceased, and after another prayer, the Chief lit the long pipe which was passed around to everyone. Custom requires everyone to take two or three puffs and pass it to his neighbor as a sign of friendship. Then before the crowd dispersed the Chief said in a loud voice: "We thank Blackrobe Pilip who came to us." And everybody replied approvingly, a, which means *yes*. I shook hands with the chiefs, said a few words of sympathy to the husband and children of Susanna, and came back. . . .

We have heard with great pleasure that another father (Father Diomedi) has requested to be assigned to these missions, and has already left Tronchiennes, they tell me, and is on his way. *Deo gratias.* [Thanks be to God.]

By the way I left out the best; do you know that the Indians ask me about you? An old man who belongs to the tribe of the Coeur d'Alenes (who speak the same language as the Flathead Indians), a few days ago asked me: "Blackrobe, is your father still alive? Is your mother alive? How many brothers do you have? Are they also Blackrobes?["]⁹ I wondered about all that solicitousness and warmth: finally when the old Indian deemed it the right moment, he added: I don't have any more tobacco for my pipe! I wouldn't have believed that the communication skills of an Indian could be so artful. I gave him the tobacco and asked him to pray for my father, my mother, siblings, and relatives. With all his heart he answered a.

I end with greetings for everyone, embracing each of you warmly. Many wishes to the fathers and brothers scattered everywhere etc. etc.

Goodbye, goodbye, goodbye,
All yours
Philip S.J., Apostolic Missionary.

[14]

Attitudes of the Indians

Stevensville, June 3, 1874

P. C.

Dearest Parents and all relatives,

I don't know if I can reply to everyone; I would like to address at least a few lines to each of you as proof of the pleasure you have given me. Today I'll have to settle for this: later, little by little, I will write a longer letter to each of you. The past few days there has been an avalanche of letters.

The first was yours of April 6 which I got May 11. With pleasure I saw all the letters: Dad, Mother, Luigi, Anna Maria, Francesco, Stanislao, Paolo, Errico: in short the whole Leonina street. – Thanks for your wishes for my Saint's day.¹ I celebrated a Mass to thank you and I hope God will recompense you a hundred times more.

While I was reading your letter, a Native by the name of Paul came into my room and said: "Blackrobe, what's that piece of red paper with those black marks you are looking at?" – I replied that my relatives from very far away sent me those black marks to give me news of them with those marks. The Indian said: *a* (I understand). And then guess what he added? Blackrobe I want to tell you something: when you make black marks like these and send them to your father and mother, make a few extra black marks and say this:

Pol S'ei zui sellagts Pilip

Coeur d'Alene Paul is a friend of Pilip. (He is from the Coeur d'Alene tribe.)

So your father and mother will see those black marks and will say: *a* Paul, the Coeur d'Alene, is a friend of Pilip's! – They will be pleased about that: That is what he said. – Did you expect to receive proof of such affection even from the Coeur d'Alenes? Yet this is how it is, and that's not all.

A week ago old Agnes from the Flathead tribe (but originally from the tribe of the Snakes), asked me out of the blue: "Pilip, have you got a mother? I answered yes, thank God. – What's her name? – Agnes: – Agnes? Oh! like myself!" That's all that was said at the time. Today I went to visit a few Indian lodges. While I was sitting on the floor on a buffalo hide, old Agnes says: "Pilip let your mother know that my name is Agnes like hers, and ask her to pray for me and tell her I will pray for her!"

I assure you that I could hardly believe my ears: such subtlety seemed so new to me coming from an Indian woman. And still that's what happened.

I am in excellent health and very happy. The Lord is helping me quite a bit as far as the language is concerned. These days I am here by myself, because the two fathers had to travel, one went some 130 miles away, the other about 28 miles, and I had to keep the ship afloat by myself. Well, I managed to do it, and I feel doubly strong with God's help.

I embrace you with all my heart: stay good and happy in our Lord, as the more we do for him, the happier we are ourselves.

Your most affectionate son

Philip S.J., Apostolic Missionary.

Beliefs of the Indians

Stevensville, June 12, 1874

P. C.

Dear Luigi,

Little by little I have to answer all the letters I got for [the feast of] St. Philip. A few days ago I wrote a few words to Dad and Mother: but that isn't enough. You see, you gave me great pleasure having [your letter] come all this way. Today I'm also writing Uncle Gioacchino Butironi. I'll tell him about a few nice little trips I've taken of late: and what will I tell you? Do you want to hear about some of the customs of our Indians? Today I'll tell you about a few of what we would call rules of Indian etiquette. I have to state in advance that a primitive and patriarchal culture is found among these tribes, so don't be surprised if you don't find them to be fashioned after the Parisian way. The curtsies, ceremonies, and formalities of our visits are just unknown here.

I think I've already told you that our whole house consists of one wooden room on the ground floor: imagine for a moment that you are a *Blackrobe*, or the Missionary at Saint Mary's. One day you are in your room, reading or writing. Someone from the outside opens the door and comes in.

Who is it? An Indian. Just as he came in without saying anything, again without saying anything he just sits down where he pleases in your room. He takes a chair or he lies down on the floor in front of you, or behind you, facing wherever he wants to, just as if you weren't there. They never say right at the beginning for what reason they've come: for a little while they don't say anything: in fact, if you ask what they want just when they come in, you can be sure that they answer *ta*, which means *nothing*. They might have come to get married or because their father or mother is about to die, but they still answer *ta*. So you just continue to read or write as if no one were in your room; do as you please as they do as they please, or else you can talk about whatever you want to, and just wait until *the toad comes out*, as the Romans say, because you can be sure they've come for some reason.

Finally after half an hour, an hour of wasted time the Native interrupts you and says: come, there is someone dying! Maybe it's shyness, or maybe to wait before asking is the proper way of doing it, the fact is that's what they do. I remember having read something similar in Homer about the heroes of that time, who having entered a tent or a military camp, first they ate, and then they were asked or they told why they had come. Everything in due time! The same manners employed coming in are used when leaving, that is to say, the Indian gets up at once and leaves your room silent like a dog. If he asked for something, a coin, a bit of tobacco, some potatoes, whatever: you give it to him, he takes it, and he goes: *Thank you, oh how nice: Your Reverence has a heart of gold!* What! That's unheard of, such words are useless around here. If, vice versa an Indian gives something to you, you do the same, and are not expected to say – Thank you. – One of the good qualities of these tribes is the right to be hosted which is so vigorously practiced among them. Every Indian who is away from his home, or even if he just feels like it, can go to sleep and eat at another one's home, without any ceremony going inside other than to lift the hide that covers the entrance and sitting down or lying down wherever he pleases. At mealtime meat will be set in front of him as if he belonged there, and he can stay as long as he pleases, days, weeks, months: then when he feels like it, he'll go out, get on his horse and leave without thanking anyone, without even saying he is leaving and not coming back.

I gave you a few bits about their visiting customs: if I started to talk about their eating and cooking habits, you could feel what refinements there are! But let's leave this for some other time. I realize I've been writing for quite some time and the hour of the Catechism is approaching. Let me add one more thing about visits, namely the custom of the pipe.

It doesn't happen that an Indian enters a lodge without the head of the lodge or someone else preparing the pipe, lighting it, taking three or four tokes, and then passing it around to everybody who is inside the lodge. So the same pipe passes through everybody's mouth, and the more the pipe goes around the more the pipe seems to smoke and the better to taste?! Earlier the one to light the pipe and smoke it had to lift the pipe and blow a puff of smoke toward the sky, then toward the East, and finally toward the West, to honor the Sun, the earth, the morning, and the evening. The other day an Indian who is already a Christian repeated the old custom just for fun, and everybody burst out laughing because now they themselves are the first ones to laugh about their earlier blindness.

All yours

Philip S.J., Apostolic Missionary.

[16]

Dress, Living Arrangements, and Foods of the Missionaries

Stevensville, June 27, 1874

P. C.

Dearest Parents,

. . .

What clothes do we wear?

This I really cannot describe. Usually in the house and around the house we wear a cassock of some kind because around here everything is good enough. Then if we go farther, where there are whitemen,[1] we dress like laymen, that is to say, like country bumpkins. The first time I saw Father Superior, I took him for one of our farmer brothers and asked him, are you the brother who takes care of the land? He answered: No: I am the Superior. – Ah, I am sorry Father! And we both had a good laugh. – Usually our clothes are ordered ready-made because we don't have any brothers who are tailors: if they tear we mend them ourselves as well as we can, or we give them to one of the more accomplished Indian women. The other day one of them brought me back a pair of trousers the underside of which had torn while I was getting on a horse. It was that pair from Brussels (tight as was the fashion), not being fit for such maneuvers, they right away cried.[2] So this Native woman held them for a while and studied at length how to fix this break. Then she brought them back sewn in such a way that I would like to send them to Anna Maria and Ersilia as a model from which they could all learn. In short, the thing was done so well that every time I sat down I could feel something like a cord underneath which reminded me where the repair was. After a few days they tore again, and since I didn't want to test the sewing woman's skill a second time, I gave the trousers to an Indian and told him they came from far away, and he was very happy to have them.

2nd When one travels the bed is just anywhere there is room to spread a buffalo hide and sleep. In the house we have some kind of mattress, good woolen blankets from California, and buffalo hides. It's clear that one doesn't talk about sheets – I haven't seen any since December. But sleep is excellent all the same, I don't know of any night that I missed it because I was between blankets half-dressed.

3rd As far as food goes, it is better than what I could expect. Beef, pork, mutton, etc., and magnificent fish, big and delicious. We have a little garden where we planted greens, peas, onions, garlic, beans, celery, etc.

I know nothing about the partridges you brought up, I haven't seen any around here. There is a great number of wild ducks and chickens. – Then we have some chickens and cows. In short, don't think we are so miserable. The beverages comprise coffee, tea, and fresh water, but really fresh. The fishing of salmon is famous with these Indians, and they are abundant in the Columbia River.

I shouldn't tell you to remember to pray to God for me so that I may measure up to the graces God has given me in the form of betterment for these poor people.

I embrace you with all my heart. – Goodbye.

Your most affectionate Son

Philip S.J.

[17]

Mission to the Canadian Kootenai Tribe

[Extracts of a Letter from the Rev. Father Rappagliosi of the Society of Jesus, Missioner in the Rocky Mountains.]

. . . On the 29th July, 1874, I left the residence at Stevensville-Saint-Mary (Idaho), for the Mission of St. Ignatius of Kalispels, situated a little more than seventy miles away.[1] The Rev. Father Superior had invited me for the Feast of St. Ignatius, which this year was transferred to Sunday, the 2nd August. On that day, I had the joy of giving Holy Communion to the Indians, and was affected even to tears on seeing the fervor with which they received their Divine Lord. On the same day, two Indians arrived, belonging to the Kootenai tribe. They were sent by their chief, and had traveled two hundred miles in search of the Blackrobe. They told us that their whole camp, and some especially who were sick, looked out for us anxiously.

This tribe, numbering more than twelve hundred souls, is divided into four camps, separated several days' journey from one another, and in an uncultivated country. The camps are called after their respective chiefs, Abraham, Joseph, David, Ignatius. The three first are much more to the north, beyond the line, traced some years ago, between the possessions of the United States and those of England. Although they are all Catholics, these Indians have not had a resident Missioner. In 1845, they were visited by Father DeSmet, and afterward by some other Fathers, who did not stay long among them, on account of the extent of the country they had to minister in.

Father Bandini and I were appointed to evangelize the Kootenais. Our baggage was soon got ready, consisting of tents, blankets, buffalo-skins, a portable altar, meal, salted provisions, and everything requisite for a long journey in a desert land.

We set out on the morning of the 3rd August, in company with two of the Indians, and traveled about fifty miles a day. On the first day, we got over thirty miles on the plain which extends to the Lake of the Flatheads. This lake is more than forty miles long. There are seven or eight islands in it: two of them are rather large, and the Indians hunt on them in various ways, and even with horses, when the lake is frozen. The Hanging-Ears River, which falls into the Columbia, flows through the lake.[2] There is a great quantity of fish in these waters.

We crossed the lake in a boat, at its narrowest breadth. The two Indians made their horses swim, and our steeds followed the lead. About seven o'clock in the evening, we pitched our tent in a spot fifteen miles from the lake, and, after a frugal supper, lay down wrapped in our blankets, and passed a very good night.

We resumed our journey at daybreak, and before long we met two Indian families, who came to shake hands with us. Immediately afterward, we entered the woods. Some families, living several leagues beyond, got notice of our expedition from one of our companions;[3] and in the evening, as we were encamped near a torrent, the Indians, men, women, and children, arrived on horseback, to have the consolation of paying their respects to a Blackrobe. They were of David's tribe, and about twenty in number. When they had joined in our prayers, they lighted fires and remained for the night.

On the evening of the third day, one of our companions started off to give notice of our arrival to the chief. An Indian offered himself as an escort on our journey. We had still one half of the distance to accomplish. After some hours traveling, we entered a wood, and soon found ourselves stumbling at every step over trees that had fallen right across the path. About two o'clock, although we had neither water for ourselves nor grass for our horses, fatigue and hunger obliged us to halt. Having eaten some wild fruit, we continued our route. At length, toward evening, we arrived on the shores of a magnificent lake. Our Indians began forthwith to fish, and being successful, we had a very good supper. To frighten away the wolves and bears, we kindled a great fire.

Issuing out of the forest on the fourth day, after accomplishing sixty miles, we found ourselves in a vast plain. In the evening we reached the camp. We dismounted, and had to shake hands with every one of the Indians, drawn up in a long line. First in order came the chief, and he gave us the sad news that one of the sick people had died that very day. We went to the tent of the deceased, who had greatly wished to see us and had testified the most sincere delight when he heard we were coming. In the morning, when by order of the chief the camp had been removed some miles nearer the church, the poor man insisted on two of the Indians taking him on their shoulders and laying him down at our feet. This holy impatience was the cause of his death; for he had hardly arrived at the church when he expired.[4]

We visited all the sick, while the chief assembled his people for prayer. The devotions having been brought to a conclusion, the notables of the tribe met together in our tent. The chief expressed the happiness they all felt in seeing the Blackrobes, and begged us to teach his subjects the true road to Heaven. While the meeting was sitting, one of the Indians presented to the chief a long pipe, which went the round of the company. I was so forgetful as to pass it to the right, instead of sending it on to the left, and the mistake excited a general laugh.

After prayers and Mass, on the morning of the 7th August, preparations were made for the burial of the deceased; and in the evening the whole tribe accompanied the remains to the cemetery. The ceremony being concluded, the property of the deceased, that is to say, his rosary and his whip, were brought to the chief. You must know that the poor man had been appointed by the chief to inflict punishment, under his orders, on guilty parties. It is the custom of the Indians, on the death of the person who has held this office, to bring the whip to the chief, who proceeds to name his successor.

The camp is literally one family, so implicit is the obedience rendered to the chief. We had nothing but praise to bestow, so great was the eagerness shown to be instructed in religion.[5] Our tent was always full of people. Four times a day they came to learn the catechism, and twice a day they assembled for prayer. It was most consoling to see them before they entered the church, going up and kissing the foot of a cross which had been erected some years ago by a Missioner. At the door, and inside the church, the chief had stationed guards with a rod in their hand, and if any of the congregation fell asleep, or showed signs of distraction, they were speedily aroused to attention by a touch of the rod. The women were on one side, and the men on the other. The chief began the prayers kneeling near the altar.

On the evening of the 7th August, three Indians arrived on horseback from the camp of Joseph, situated eighty miles farther on. They came to entreat us not to leave without visiting their camp also. One of them, the chief second in rank, a venerable old man, named Moses, was the first to enter our tent, and when he had been presented with a pipe, he began to tell us that there were a great many sick in the camp, besides the old people, who could not undertake the journey, and that all were anxious to go to confession. Our answer was to the effect that we should go there as soon as we had finished the visitation of the camp of David. Old Moses pressed our hand in token of satisfaction, and next morning one of the envoys set out to carry the good tidings to the camp.

We remained two days longer, teaching catechism, hearing confessions, and preparing children for first Communion. On the morning of the general Communion, all, with tears in their eyes, approached the Holy Table. There was no external splendor, no solemn pomp; nothing but simple faith to excite their devotion. Afterward I baptized five infants a few months old, the only ones who had not already received the sacrament of regeneration. Although the Missioner had not made his appearance there for many years, all the other children had been carried a great distance to the Blackrobe by their mother. The mother of one of these five infants had herself arrived that very day, after a long journey. Another ceremony was the erection of a cross in the middle of the cemetery. We had previously gone with the chief and some of his men to a neighboring wood, to cut down the largest pine-tree that could be got. The Indians made a great cross of it, which they carried on their shoulders to the cemetery, where it was blessed in sight of the whole camp.

On the morning of the 10th August, we left our good Indians, and took our way to the camp of David [sic, should be Joseph]; but we had to promise to call to see them again on our return, and the chief forbade any of his people to set out on the buffalo-hunt until the Blackrobe had come back. We took our departure, accompanied by old Moses and seven or eight other Indians, on horseback and well armed, under the command of the chief David. Rain fell incessantly all day.

Next evening, we arrived on the banks of a great river.[6] An Indian was to have come to take us over in a canoe. These canoes are nothing more than the bark of a tree with the ends turned over. Two, three, or four persons can sit in one of them. As the bark is thin, it is covered over with little pieces of wood plaited together. One has to use the utmost precaution stepping into this frail skiff, and to remain on board sitting on one's heels. The Indian whom we expected to take us over was slow in making his appearance; but at length he heard the shots fired off by our companions, showed himself on the opposite bank, and presently, ascending the stream, came up to us in his little boat. He took over, first our baggage, then the Indians, three at a time, and lastly the two Blackrobes. The horses swam across the stream.

By this time we were close to the camp, and as soon as our companions descried the tents, they fired off three or four shots. The Indians of the camp returned the salute by a still greater number. The Kootenais of this district are encamped, not in the plain, but in a wood.

First came the chief Joseph, and after him all the others, to shake hands with us.[7] Meanwhile, some of them brought great trunks of trees close to our tent, and lighted a great fire to warm us; for, though it is the 11th August, snow has fallen on the mountains in the vicinity. In the evening, an old Indian came to visit us, having on his arm the marks of a wound received by the bite of a wolf, which he afterward killed. In allusion to this, they have given him an Indian name, signifying "Wolf's ornament."[8] As it was perceived that we listened to his narrative with interest, four or five others came to show us their wounds also, and to relate their battles and their victories, the trophies of which they wear round their necks in the form of collars, the pearls being the teeth of the animals they had killed. By-and-by the signal for prayer was given. The church was constructed that very day, of some few stakes covered with branches and skins, four staves bound together supporting our little altar. The Indians, much more numerous here than in David's camp, assemble with the greatest exactitude for Mass and instruction. On the twelfth, other parties of Indians arrived at the camp. We had catechism classes four times a day.

On the night of the thirteenth, arrived two Indians from Abraham's camp, which is distant at least four days' journey. Next morning, the envoys confessed and received Holy Communion, and then set off again with old Moses.[9] Paul Ignatius, called the Thunderer, chief of the Signeses, sent two Indians to invite us to visit them; but his camp lay too far off, and we were obliged to refuse.[10]

Ten children were baptized on Sunday and we blessed some marriages. Not a single Indian was missing at the general Communion. Even the youngest children went to confession. On the fifteenth of August, we parted from the good Indians to return to David's camp, where we arrived on the evening of the seventeenth. Some marriages were blessed on the twentieth.[11]

Rappagliosi, S.J.
Missioner at the Rocky Mountains.

[18]

Hardships of Winter in These Missions

Saint Ignatius [January] 18th of 1875

P. C.

Dearest Parents and relatives.

We are now in the new year which arrived here very cold, with hats and I don't know how many Lucca blankets on.[1] The fact is that as soon as it arrived, we started to say: goodness, what cold! and this is the first news item I have to give you: for a few weeks now we have been in full winter, hard winter, Rocky Mountain winter.[2] Thank goodness our little wooden house is equipped with good chimneys and iron stoves, with good hides and blankets, but in spite of all this, cold still manages to stick its nose inside, and that nose is so powerful that for all the nice fire we have in our little rooms in the morning we still find the water frozen in the bucket, the ink frozen in the inkstand, and that beautiful fire seems more a painted fire. In the Church it's even worse: we have a nice stove, we even put the fire on the altar; you might not believe it, but with all this, the chalice still freezes during Mass, even twice during Mass. We have been forced to celebrate it in the bedroom now. The whole country is covered with snow, the rivers and creeks are solid like a piece of marble. Though the Indians are used to it, they still come and gather around our stoves, and as I write there is a whole circle of them here chattering and smoking so that I hardly know what it is I am writing. I keep the inkstand in hot water, but still the cold finds a way of making fun of me, because the ink freezes in my pen mid-word, and there I am staring at it wide-eyed. But this isn't the worst of it: soon we will hear that more than one of these poor people has died of the cold or has ended up without feet or hands. Last night a poor woman came knocking at Father Bandini's door. It was one-thirty at night. She was weeping, saying, come, come: my old father is half frozen to death: we found him an hour ago far from home, stretched out on the snow, motionless. We carried him home and laid him near the fire; the first thing he said after he regained consciousness is that he wanted to go to confession.

The Father went there at once and gave him confession: then the old man asked for something warm to drink: as soon as he had drunk he fell back dead, most certainly done in by the too quick change from cold to hot.[3] Instead of warming him gradually, the Indians had used remedies which were too fast and too violent for the state he was in. As I have said, I feel such pity for these poor people, half naked and in their miserable hide lodges.

As for us, we are surviving pretty well, and we do feel the cold, but more than feeling it we see it.

I am in excellent health, and spent Christmas busy, but I am satisfied with the work of the Mission which (as I already wrote to you in December) we have had to do for the various little tribes here gathered....

. . .

Enough for today: I have written a typical January letter and all I talked about was the cold. Be patient because there is a good supply of it. Goodbye. I embrace you with all my heart.

Your most affectionate

Philip, Apostolic Missionary, S.J.

[19]

Death of a Young Indian

Saint Ignatius, February 27, 1875

P. C.

Dearest Parents and relatives,

There is no regular postal service at Saint Ignatius where I am now, and when there is an opportunity we have to send our letters to the nearest post office forty-five miles away.[1] So I'm writing this today, and God only knows when it can be sent off. The letters that come to us, too, we can send for when there is an opportunity and at this time of the year it's hard to find an opportunity. We are cut off by the snow. Last time I wrote to you was January, but my letter left many days later. Even then I was telling you about the cold we are having this year. But it's lessening now and this letter will be proof for you that Pippo isn't frozen.

I answered your last letter dated November. I haven't received any others since then. I believe that since I moved to a different residence, the letters you wrote since November have either gotten lost, or else they are waiting at the post office where we pick up our mail only when we can.

As you see, you and I have to be patient and let winter pass and the snow melt. In fair seasons our letters don't take longer than a month and when (as now) at the end of February I read news of you from mid-November, one month seems quite short.

Here now some news.

After the Mission had been given to the Natives they spread in all directions; some went fishing, others deer hunting. Nevertheless a certain number always stay around the church, and I do the Catechism with them three times a day. As I have said to you several times, I am in their midst like a father or brother, to tell you what I feel in my heart. This week we have had several deaths. I felt sorrow at the loss of a young married man.[2] I tried to help him to the last. He suffered terribly, and it broke my heart to see him writhing on a buffalo hide on the ground. I found some straw and although he couldn't speak much he showed much gratitude for that bit of relief. His old father said to me: Blackrobe, this is the last son I have left, I've lost all the others, either to sickness or they were killed in war with other tribes. But God who is our master, will do according to his will and although I will weep if he takes him back from me, still I say: You have given him to me, you have taken him back: he is in better hands with you than with me. – These are the words of the old father without any changes. Then he suggested to his son devotional thoughts and oaths. When he died, we immediately said a few prayers with the Indians who were present, and then, as custom requires, the terrible wailings began. I say custom because they signal when to start and when to stop, and they mix them with suffocating cries, which for us are at the same time a pain and a scene to watch. The fact is that this time I was more moved because I had seen all that had come before and I knew the pain of this poor old man, which, though shown in the Indians' way, was still the pain of a father.

Someone has just entered my room, saying that my letter can leave today. So, I prefer to finish the letter the way it is, instead of waiting for who knows when the next opportunity comes. It doesn't matter much that it is not long. It suffices for you to know that all the snow and cold of these mountains brings me excellent appetite, and my health is excellent. I hope this is the case for all of you, too. I always pray for you, and it is as if I always were among you, and we were always united in our prayers and in the sacrifice God asked us to do and which we do with all our hearts. Goodbye. I embrace you affectionately.

Yours forever

Philip S.J., Apostolic Missionary.

[20]

Dealings with an Indian Chief

[Another letter of Philip Rappagliosi from April 14, 1875, makes us familiar with the difficulty which missionaries among the Indians must face frequently, namely the moodiness, touchiness, and small-minded vanity of the chiefs. The ability of the Father to appease and to win over the offended chief and the picture of Indian ways of life that is presented to us at this occasion leads us to submit this letter to our readers. – 1876 editor of *Katholischen Missionen.*]

Since I wrote my last letter, I spent two weeks in another Indian camp to teach those who were making their first communion.[1] The chief of that camp had been angry at us for some time. He is a very eloquent (in Indian terms) and extremely proud man; some Whites and Protestants or Catholics (in name only) used this to change his mind about us. As a result of recent contracts between the government of the United States and his tribe, he received much money since part of the Indian land was ceded. This caused him to become conceited so that he became demanding and unmalleable. Therefore my trip had two purposes: I wanted to teach the children about the Catechism, and to win back the heart of that stubborn Indian and his people. When I arrived at the camp he was not there; but I knew that he would have to return the day after and this was exactly what happened. Our first talk was rather cold, especially in the beginning. When I got off my horse in front of his cabin, he was by coincidence standing by the door and looked at me as if he did not know me. I went over, shook his hand, and welcomed him back. He turned his head away and gave no answer. Pretending not to have realized, I continued: "I am coming to visit you." Then he waved me over into his house and said: "Come in!" I entered and saw two women who offered me a big wooden chair.² I believed that this was the throne of the ruler of the Indians, who was still standing angrily outside. Therefore, I only took a seat on a little bench. After some minutes the chief came in too and immediately sat down on the big armchair. I was very happy that I had left it free. Then I told him that I had come to teach those who were making their first Communion, and that I was going to stay in the camp for a couple of days. He did not pay attention to this and started right away to express his anger about something that had happened to him with one of the Blackrobes. I already knew about the whole story and had expected this eruption. That's why I patiently let him speak and, when I realized that he was about to get to the end of his expressions of anger, I calmly said: "I appreciate your opening your heart to me; but maybe we should talk about it another time. I will come back. Today I just wanted to come for a short while and now I will head back to the one who offered shelter to me for tonight." And, putting my hand on his shoulder, I whispered into his ear as if he were my best friend: "I want to stay and eat with you too a couple of times for as you know I do not have a residence here." He answered calmly, "Oh!" which meant good. This "Oh" was not unimportant to me, but being content with my first visit, I climbed up on my horse with the hope that the "Oh" would be followed by what still needed to be said.

Two days later I was back and the reception was much friendlier. He shook my hand, had me sit down on his chair, and passed me the pipe — the strongest sign of friendship among the Indians. Then he said to me: "Philip, I love you," and added a flattering compliment about my knowledge and pronunciation of the Indian language. I used this moment of good humor to tell him that I had not eaten since the early morning. At once he had a good meal prepared for me. In order to honor me he wanted me to eat by myself, but I realized that he would rather eat with me. Then he took a seat next to me and called for three or four others of the best educated to join us. After

Father Philip Rappagliosi, S.J. Undated photograph
by M. A. Eckert, Helena, Montana Territory. Courtesy
Jesuit Oregon Province Archives, Gonzaga University,
Spokane, Washington (negative 1027.02).

Father Philip Rappagliosi, S.J. Undated photograph by
O. C. Bundy, Virginia City, Montana Territory. Courtesy Montana
Historical Society, Helena (photograph 943-755).

Father Joseph Guidi, S.J., ca. 1885. Guidi had been Rappagliosi's friend in Italy and was his fellow missionary in the Rocky Mountain Missions and, finally, his biographer. Photographer unknown. Courtesy Jesuit Oregon Province Archives, Gonzaga University, Spokane, Washington (negative 1026.01a).

St. Mary's Mission in the Bitterroot Valley. Undated photograph by
Rollin McKay. Courtesy McKay Collection, K. Ross Toole Archives,
The University of Montana-Missoula (photograph 94-94).

St. Ignatius Mission on the Flathead Indian Reservation, 1865.
Watercolor by Peter Tofft. Courtesy Montana Historical
Society, Helena (catalog number X62.05.01).

Old St. Peter's Mission near Birdtail Rock. Undated photograph
by R. E. DeCamp. Courtesy Montana Historical Society,
Helena (photograph 950-778).

Charlo, chief of the Bitterroot Salish during the 1870s. Detail from
Delegation of Flathead Indians, Washington DC, 1884. Photograph by
John K. Hillers, Bureau of American Ethnology, Washington DC.
Courtesy Montana Historical Society, Helena (photograph 954-526).

Chief Arlee of the Bitterroot Salish living on the Flathead Reservation
in the 1870s, undated drawing. From Peter Ronan, *Historical
Sketch of the Flathead-Indians from the Year 1813 to 1890*
(Helena MT: Journal Publishing Co., 1890), 78.

the meal we sat down around the fireplace again. Quietly and cere-moniously we lit the pipe and passed it around in the circle. As soon as the first clouds of smoke had begun dancing in the air the chief interrupted the silence and spoke: "Blackrobe, when the Indian has finished a meal with his friends he smokes, and when he smokes he talks about what he wants." I saw what this whole introduction was aiming at. I answered: "Oh!" and he repeated the whole of his angry speech from two days before. The thing was like this: At Christ-mas a Mission had been completed for the Indians which ended at Epiphany or Three Kings Day. Because the Indians were still on the hunt it was impossible to gather them earlier. On Christmas Eve, as usual, a long ceremonious service took place with many Indian par-ticipants. The Father who held Mass, however, recommended they postpone Communion until the end of the Mission, although he al-lowed people to take Communion during this Holy Night if they wished. My chief arrived just the night before Christmas and went to the Father in order to confess and take Communion. The Father gave him the Sacraments but then he made the comment that all the other chiefs had preferred to wait until the end of the Mission to prepare themselves more fully, and that he would have done better to wait as well. Haughtily he went away swearing about everything.

When he started complaining to me, he asked why Christmas had not been celebrated with the tribe of Saint Ignatius this year. I re-plied to him and said that it had been celebrated and that I had gathered the people at midnight, decorated and lit up the church, and that there had been a Christ Child on the altar, etc. Hypocriti-cally he threw in that Christmas had not been celebrated because there had not been any Communion. I responded: "Everybody who wanted to could take Communion." He answered: "But the Father refused to give it to me." "The Father did not refuse," I said, "but he told you what he told everybody else as well, namely, to wait until the end of the Mission to become more fully prepared." He did not know what to say now and seemed to be satisfied. Then he started to ask me other random questions which were not his own ideas but had been taught to him in an evil manner by the Whites. I slowly answered all of them, and when he had nothing else to say anymore I spoke to all the bystanders and reminded them to keep the faith. When I had finished they said all together: "We agree." Since it was already nighttime we prayed and everybody went to sleep. Early in the morning I went away to hold Mass in the cabin of a sick man as I had promised. I, nevertheless, informed the chief of the fact that I would celebrate Mass at his place next Sunday and that's where the Indians should be gathered. That placated his ego quite well, and I took the chance to offer him the Sacrament of Confession. During the week I continued teaching Catechism. On Saturday I returned to the chief; he received me in a friendly fashion and confessed as did several others after him. The conversation during the evening went on very amicably and no angry word was said. On Sunday morning the Indians gathered and the chief and the others took Communion. When I said goodbye the chief shook my hand, affirmed his contentedness to me, and promised to come to the mission church at Easter — a promise that cheered me up and gave evidence of the fact that I had won him back completely. He kept his word and visited the other Fathers also. All the ones whom I had prepared for their first Communion came with him. They all received their first Communion at the biggest feast of the ecclesiastical year.

[21]

Devotion of the Indians to Holy Mary

Saint Ignatius, May 10, 1875

P. C.

Dearest Parents,

Finally the good season has started here, too! The snow has vanished at least in the valleys and two weeks ago we started to plow and sow seeds. The earth is greening and the trees are getting leaves. May, which is the month of the Virgin and of the flowers, is giving us a few flowers here and there, but few. Speaking of May, several days ago I started to put together an exhibit of the gifts the Indians had made to Mary at the time of the last mission. The icon and the

painting of Our Lady are covered with these gifts. Mary, our good
Mother, had to put up with looking like a good Indian with all the
things we put on her: because, you should know, that while we give
as gifts things of gold and silver, precious stones and gems, these
good Indians give all kinds of trinkets. Therefore the Holy Virgin
of Saint Ignatius has a peculiar collection of gifts. On her chest a
beautiful seashell necklace, then strands of stringed multicolored
glass beads highlighted now and then by a big wolf's tooth or some
bear claws and similar objects. Around the painting there are gar-
ments, belts, scarves, shoes, brass or iron bracelets, mirrors, little
chains, buttons, and such objects of all kinds which the Indians had
gotten from the Whitemen and hadn't known before. To straighten
out all these treasures (or this heap of junk as we Romans would
say) I need a lot of patience. Among the other gifts I found a coffee
spoon and tin cup which were hard for me to arrange nicely. Turned
this way, turned that way, they still looked like a tin cup and a coffee spoon! I had just finished arranging everything, and gone back
to the Church, where I found an Indian standing on a bench, busy
pinning his offering with much devotion. It was a *pottery shard and
three matches*, and he had pinned them right in the Virgin's ear! Then
he cocked his head to the side and stared as if to say: "*Yes, they look
good!*" – But the nicest gifts that I made sure were more visible than
anything else, are some objects of superstition and almost of idolatry of which the Natives had deprived themselves out of love for the
Virgin. A few of them, not too many, they kept them after they had
been baptized [i.e., after they had become Christians], if not with
the same veneration, at least with some affection: things which the
Fathers had rightly thought of as of the devil. So they offered even
such things to the Virgin, and thus they came to place the devil at
the Holy Virgin's feet. These superstitious items usually consist of
feathers or birds' beaks, animal teeth or skins, or certain herbs or
plants. They bring them wrapped up in little rags, and especially in
former times they considered them as holy. – We have started the
month of Mary here, too, and we hope that Holy Mary will have,
if not from the earth, at least from our hearts, her flowers and her
crown.

As I wrote to you in my last letter, it won't be long before I go to my new assignment among the Blackfeet Indians. The General Superior will accompany me and I think we will leave after Pentecost....

. . .

Enough for today: Goodbye, Goodbye: I embrace you all heartily. I always pray for you, and please remember me and my dear Indians.[1] All yours
Philip S.J., Apostolic Missionary.

[22]

St. Peter's Mission at the Blackfeet

Saint Peter, July 27, 1875

P. C.

Dearest Parents and relatives,

Here I am in Saint Peter. That's a great reward for a Roman. But this Saint Peter is a bit different from the one in Rome. The Palace and the Basilica here consist of two cabins made with logs and mud, with a roof covered with earth: each of the two cabins is nothing but one room on a ground floor. The square is our field, and the colonnade that circles everything in our little valley is the mountains and the hills. These mountains look strange: the slopes have nice meadows, but the peaks are crowned with rocks and precipitous boulders variously shaped. The mountains get their names from the various figures that these boulders suggest from a distance: there is in fact the *Birdtail*, the *Beartooth*, the *Saddlehorn*, the *Finger*, the *Fish*, and whatnot....

We arrived Friday, twenty-third of this month, day consecrated to the Holy Heart of Jesus. Our arrival was met with a circumstance which we took as a good omen.

The General Superior Father Giorda had promised some months ago that he would have ordered from New York two beautiful statues of the Virgin and of Saint Joseph if the Blackfeet Mission could be opened. In order to move our two celestial protectors he sent away for the statues before it was decided that the Mission should be reopened. And here the two statues are delivered the very same day we arrived. The following Sunday we installed them, that is to say in one of the two cabins which I mentioned above, and that for the time being serves both as a chapel and a bedroom. In the middle we placed the painting of Saint Peter, the Mission's namesake, which had been sent to us by our Father General.

The climate here is, as everywhere in the Rocky Mountains, excellent, we are in perfect solitude, because, as I've told you before, although this is called a Mission, it is more than anything else the missionaries' residence; but the real Mission is in the Indians' camps that we must visit, and that are spread all over this vast Blackfeet country. Our poor house and the nearby field is the place where, after the above-mentioned visits among the Indians, the missionary finds some peace for body and mind.

At some distance from here there are a few mixed-blood families. In the house we are two fathers, two brothers, and two workers. For now my occupation is to study that other language. I started immediately Sunday twenty-fifth of this month: as I wrote to you when I was among the Flatheads that they say *gest sgalgalt* for *good day*, now I tell you that the Blackfeet say *arsi ksistikui*. Just looking at this simple example you can see how similar these languages are, right? Later, if you like, I'll give you more compliments in Blackfeet. The first thing I am studying now is the prayers. Just out of curiosity I copy the Hail Mary for you.

Hail Mary full of grace with thee is
Kiarpiksistatòrsit Mania, irtuitsiu arsii, kitorpukopiim
the Lord all women thou art chosen among Jesus your son
Apistotòkiu: kanauàkiiks tsitaapsàtsima; Jesus kurkùa
is blessed Holy Mary of God Mother
tsitaapsàtsima. — Santa Mania, Apistotòkiu uksìstsi
pray for us sinners now and when we are near
atsimoikartòmokit, makapsi annùrk, aesturkimmìniki,
to die. Amen.
tsitaaksinnìsi. Kamumanirtòpi.

As you may have observed, the Blackfeet don't have the letter r so they cannot say Mary, and they say Mania. They have neither l nor f: so the Flatheads said Pilip, but here the Blackfeet say Pinip.

The letter r which occurs frequently in the Hail Mary, as you've seen, isn't really r, but is meant to indicate a guttural sound which you can't express other than by saying it and which is very similar to the German g and the Spanish j, or here, among the Indian languages, to the g of the Kalispels. I just told you all this to show you that I am really involved in the study of this language, but for the rest it's not necessary for me to go into more details.

We don't have a post office here: when we can we have to send our letters fifteen miles to where there is a military fort called Fort Shaw.[1] We rarely get a chance: so don't be surprised if you notice delays in my letters and don't worry. . . .

. . .

Goodbye, goodbye; be well and always thank the Lord that he called me to do a bit of good for these poor people; God has shown great mercy to me, in spite of all my unworthiness. A large part of the reward will be yours. I embrace you with all my heart.

Your son, Philip S.J. Blackrobe
Kurkuua Pinip Sikepiszi, sukasim.

[23]

Those Indians' Ways of Life and Their Superstitions

Saint Peter, November 11, 1875

P. C.

Dearest Parents,

. . . I continue to be in good health. Winter is quickly approaching and for us this is a sign to get ready to visit our Indians. We've heard that buffalo herds are coming down from the North. The Blackfeet always stay where the buffalo stay because they mean everything to them; so with the buffalo the Indians approach, too. I'll write again before I leave. In the meantime we are anxiously waiting.

I know that you continue to pray for me, and that every evening at Rosary time you recite the prayers I recommended to you. Our hopes are there, in the prayers said for us. Speaking from a human point of view we have undertaken quite a difficult task, but it is fine, and no one can boast about what will happen, and the conversion of this tribe will all be the work of God.

As I said, I am anxiously awaiting the moment when we will encounter the Natives, but I know about the sufferings awaiting us. We don't have any other means to approach them than to go among them with our tent and live with them, and follow them in their wanderings. One can easily understand what kind of a life this is: but we have the blessing of obedience, and the hope that in this way they will end up knowing God our Lord. This is why we wish, and can't help counting impatiently the days until then.[1]

...

I ask again all of you to pray for our dear tribe. May they get to know God, love and serve him and deserve to enjoy him eternally! So far they have lived in idolatry and worshipped the sun, the moon, and the earth, and they are full of superstitions. They have some ideas about the immortality of the soul, but for them Paradise isn't anything other than a faraway land covered with beautiful pastures and traveled by innumerable buffalo and deer herds where the good will live in abundance, but the evil will go to barren and desert lands, where they will starve.

This paradise full of buffalo seems such a nice thing to them that when we talk about a much more beautiful paradise they listen in wonder.

A few days ago I saw a very old woman of the Blackfeet tribe. She hadn't been baptized. She told me she was too old to receive baptism (you catch her drift). Then she told me that after her death she wanted to go with the other Indians to the far-off green meadows where the buffalo abound.

We talked for a long time, but the old woman still had in mind the *buffalo* and the *eternal hunt* and the *always green meadows*.

I end by greeting affectionately everybody at home, and embracing you with all my heart, I am

All yours

Philip, Apostolic Missionary, S.J.

[24]

Attitudes of the Indians toward Religious Instruction and the Life of the Missionaries among Them

Old Fort Maginnis, January 3, 1876

P. C.

Dearest Parents,

We left about a month ago to come here among these Indians. Although it was December, our journey on horseback was quite pleasant and after six days we arrived in the interior of Blackfeet territory. Thank God we found that these Indians are well disposed to learn prayers, that is to say to receive religious instruction. That's not insignificant, and we are sure that once they have known the sublime truths of our holy religion, God will give them grace to do the rest. Three times a day we do Catechism. The Chief himself comes out of his lodge and cries loudly that they should all come to hear the prayer.

We are very pleased they have already learned the sign of the Cross, the Our Father and the Hail Mary, and some other prayers and the principal mysteries of our Holy Faith: especially the youngsters learn easily. We also taught them a few songs. At Christmas they sang a song appropriate for the occasion, that is the *You descend from the stars King of Heaven*, etc. translated into their language.

Other Sundays they sang another one, *We are guilty of a thousand errors*, for the Holy Virgin. It makes me feel compassion and tenderness to hear these songs sung by people who are still faithless and who haven't yet experienced how sweet the doctrine of our Lord is, who became a man for our sake, and who don't know yet how many hopes lie in Saint Mary's protection. But the fact that they let others teach them, and their docility and the respect they show toward the Minister of the Lord will certainly be the beginning of their salvation.

God has so far given us good strength and health in spite of the life we have to lead. We live with the Indians in their lodges day and night. Their lodges, as you know, are some kind of a hut made out of buffalo hide; at the bottom there is a little opening which is the door: you enter on all fours, one at a time: at the top of the lodge there is another opening which serves as a chimney. A fire burns in the middle and everybody sits or lies on the hides around the fire. You can't stand up on account of all the smoke. Their main food is buffalo meat cooked their own way. But since they started to sell to the Whitemen the skins of the animals they kill, they also get flour, potatoes, and similar things, although they pay outrageous prices on account of the great distances which the few whitemen who bring them for the fur trade have to transport them.

The lodge where we have been staying belongs to one of the great chiefs named Arsapaki which means *Good-woman* in their language. He received us very well: he gave us the best place, which is opposite the door: he let us spread the hides on the floor and this is our seat and our bed, and we use our horse saddle to lay our pillow on. These tepees are very warm and one doesn't suffer the cold as one might think looking at them. They know how to make them airtight all around so that the wind hardly comes in.

Within the first few days I saw fifteen lodges of the *Pend d'Oreilles* who are the Natives among whom I stayed last year.[1] They came here to hunt. They made quite a fuss when they saw the Blackrobe again in this desert. Their presence was a good example to the Blackfeet, and they gave them much edification by approaching the Holy Sacraments with great piety and faith.

Now Father Imoda is visiting another camp: I am staying here in Arsapaki's camp. We are camped along the river they call *two lodges of Medicine.*[2] Although I am all alone among the Indians, God comforts me a lot, because he knows I do this for him. The Indians, too, show me a lot of affection. Others invite me to their lodges to eat

with them, which among them is proof of friendship and hospitality. A certain Orkonnokim (this beautiful name means man hated
by all), sent for me one evening and the chief accompanied me to his
lodge.[3] What was the matter? They were preparing an extraordinary
dinner; instead of buffalo meat which is their usual food they had
fixed a few slices of potatoes, and they didn't want to leave out the
Blackrobe. But what pleases me most is the dedication with which
they come to learn prayers.

If you want to know the name they gave me it is quite difficult
to pronounce, but with a little practice you will manage: they call
me Ickisksesi (Aquiline-nose). Father Imoda's name is Akspinnin
(Cloven-cheek). This is the Indian custom, what we would consider a
nickname is used here with seriousness and respect: so, for example,
one might say in a sermon: tomorrow Cloven-cheek (father Imoda)
will arrive here to baptize the children, or Aquiline-nose, Round-
head (father Giorda), Left-handed (father Grassi), Blond-hair (father
D'Aste), or another of the fathers.

I send these few lines by means of an Indian, and I hope they will
arrive among the whitemen so that you will soon have some news.
Later on I will write to you a more detailed letter as I did after my
visit to the Kootenais. . . . Today I just wanted to give you some quick
news for your relief; just continue to address your letters as usual.
I will collect them at the post office when I'll go back to the whitemen. Otherwise they might get lost because I travel from one camp
to another, following the Indians.

Continue to pray for me and for this poor tribe of Indians. I say
hello and embrace you all with all my heart. May God look after you
and grant us always to fulfill his holy will which is the only reason
we are in this world. Kindest regards also to the religious fathers and
brothers. Always think of me as being with God.

Your most devoted Son
Philip S.J.

[25]

Letter from Pius IX to the Catholic Indians of St. Ignatius

Saint Peter, March 14, 1876

P. C.

Dearest Parents,

I send you the translation of a letter which our Holy Father wrote to the Indians of the Saint Ignatius Mission.[1] ...

I am in very good health. The month of March has arrived in an extraordinarily bad mood; all it brought us is snow. But April isn't too far away and at least May will give some relief to our pains.

You tell us that they don't believe that it's twenty-five degrees below zero here. But it's the truth. Even more, sometimes the centigrade thermometer drops to thirty to forty degrees below zero. The proof of this extreme cold is that almost every year the mercury in the thermometer freezes. Now it is known that mercury freezes at forty degrees.

That one can't live here isn't true. Of course, one has to take due precautions, but still one can live here. But it isn't rare for people to freeze to death. Last year the man who accompanied father Scellen froze to death and it was a miracle the father himself survived.[2] Father Scellen is an *Oblate* priest, a conscientious missionary to the Natives.[3] I have often seen people who have lost a foot, a hand, their ears, or their noses to the cold. I say all this for those who might not believe me, but don't be alarmed for me. You see that so far, thank God, I haven't lost a single hair from my head, and everything is in its place. ...

Kindest regards to each and every one of the relatives.

I embrace you with all my heart. – Goodbye.

All yours

Philip S.J., Apostolic Missionary.

To the Faithful Beloved Sons of the Mission of Saint Ignatius in the Rocky Mountains in the apostolical vicarage of Idaho.
Pope Pius IX

Beloved Sons, hail and Apostolic Blessing.

Reading your letter, dearest sons, was like returning to the apostolic times when faith and charity were so alive, that all believers were one in heart and soul. And certainly we can't have greater consolation than this, now that we are afflicted every day with the aberrations of many, who, drawn by the love of new things and new doctrines, refuse to hear the truth, and turn to fantasies, and itching to hear them, seek teachers. But if those miserable people are off of the right track, you are certainly staying on it, you who with such devotion and reverence keep close to this Rostrum of truth from where the light of the gospel has reached you. That you deplore the straying of some of your brothers demonstrates, doubtlessly, that you, too, are subject to temptation; but this is necessarily so because man's life on earth is militancy, and one demonstrates faithfulness in the face of temptation. So remain strong in the faith you have embraced, and act so that temptation works to your advantage and glory. This will not be difficult for you if you obediently listen to and accept the instructions of your missionaries, and if you faithfully follow their advice because by virtue of their bond of faith and charity with Our apostolic Vicar, they are closely connected with Us. The persistence with which you have resisted following the example of your errant brothers has made us appreciate even more the success with which you have applied yourselves and the affection you have offered as proof of your filial love toward us. But more than anything else, we have been consoled by the help of your prayers which, together with the prayers of the whole Church, alone can invoke that celestial force that both the Church, wherever it is harshly persecuted, and troubled countries, need. So persevere in prayer, beloved sons and daughters, to keep danger at bay; persevere in this for Us and for the entire Catholic family, so that our most merciful Lord, soothed by your prayers and those of His people, may grant peace at least in such troubled times. May the Holy Spirit fill you with His gifts; indeed, we desire that this take place through the Apostolic Blessing that we give to all you beloved sons and daughters and to each of your Missionaries, as proof of our paternal love.

Given in Rome, Saint Peter's, March 8, 1875
of Our Pontificate year 29
PIUS PP. IX

[26]

Mission Work among the Blackfeet and Pend d'Oreilles Indians

[According to a letter of P. Rappagliosi from March 28, 1876, we can provide the following about the progress of the mission among the Blackfeet and Pend d'Oreilles – 1876 editor of *Katholischen Missionen*.]

I spent a large part of the spring with the Blackfeet and now I want to tell you about the reason for that visit. On December 5 I went on my way to the area of the Indian camps, together with Father Imoda. The first we met were seven lodges of Blackfeet and nine lodges of Pend d'Oreilles who camped together at the mouth of the Natochiokas River.[1] The Pend d'Oreilles had come from the buffalo hunt; they belong to the St. Ignatius Mission where I stayed the winter of the year before. When they saw me again they took me into their midst and showed such a devotion that the Blackfeet became very astonished. It seemed as if God had ordained this meeting with the already converted families of Indians for the benefit of the others. We entered the lodge of the chief of the Blackfeet. He was one of the three big chiefs of the tribe and his name was Arsapaki. He had just left on the hunt this day; but he returned the following day. He showed great pleasure on seeing Father Imoda again and shook my hand; and then he gave us the best part of his bag to eat – the tongue of the buffalo.

Since they had often expressed their desire to adopt the true belief and to have a Blackrobe among them, Father Imoda told them that they would get a new Blackrobe this year. The two of us were here for them and as soon as we had baptized the children, we would start to teach all how to pray and to prepare the others for the sacrament of baptism. The chief showed his approval and when the message became known outside, the women brought their children to the

Father. This way in those seven lodges fourteen children of the age of four or five years or younger were reborn through Baptism. All came in the morning and at night to learn how to pray and the Pend d'Oreilles, who were already taught adequately, prayed loudly in their camp. In order to be able to give the signal they had brought a little bell from the mission when they left there. After the prayers the singing started; this set a good example for the Blackfeet who in their hearts soon felt the desire to sing as well. Even they learned a song within a short period of time and they sang it for Christmas. It was the song of the pious shepherd, translated into their language: "Tu scendi dalle stelle" [You have descended from the firmament]. I must confess that my heart was full of hope. This new tribe was not completely converted yet, but the voices of its people joined together in song with the others to praise the Redeemer.

Father Imoda prayed in the language of the Blackfeet. I did the same in the language of the Pend d'Oreilles. We spoke briefly during the Mass and distributed Communion. From the families of the Pend d'Oreilles, everybody who had reached the minimum age came to the Sacraments.

Due to God's providence even more Indians joined us with their great chiefs. They came to pray too. The conversation that followed the prayer united them all and resulted in even those poor Indians becoming influenced by the power of divine grace. This is really a fine beginning. Then the talk turned to the biggest difficulty – polygamy. Father Imoda told them that they did not yet know all the power of divine grace. They only needed to learn the prayers and be taught about the truth of the faith and then they would feel themselves strengthened by it.

After that these poor Indians invited us to visit their camp and to stay longer so that we could teach them. That touched us and we believe it would have touched God's heart even more. The other Indians had scattered here and there to go hunting and they had their camps along the Orso River in groups of ten or twenty families, quite a distance away from one another.[2] Since the little camp of Arsapaki was so receptive to our Catechism we finally decided not to leave it entirely. That is why we agreed to separate, and, toward the end of December, Father Imoda left me to go to the other camps while I remained with the Indians of the Natochiokas.

After the departure of my brother, I courageously started to teach and perfect those who earlier had promised to become the Catechism teachers for the others. Learning the language of the Blackfeet, which was totally different from the one of the Pend d'Oreilles, was no little difficulty. But, thank God, I did not lose my patience. With the book in my hands I read the prayers and the Catechism with a loud voice and the Indians repeated them word by word in good faith. After a certain time I received consolation from the fact that the Indians had learned them, and I, as well, had learned to recite them without the help of my book. I taught them only the Rosary, and they prayed it every night with the men and the women taking turns. They never failed to make the sign of the cross before eating and to pray in the morning and in the night. All learned to sing the song of St. Alphons in their language – "Siam rei di molti errori" [Carrying the guilt of sin] – and they sang it always at the end of the prayer.[3]

I can guarantee you that the success so far pleased me greatly and it compensated for all the effort made. Their old superstition and worship of the sun, of the moon, and of so many other things seems to have ceased to exist voluntarily. On the hunt they get off their horses, put down their weapons, and pray the Our Father. As soon as they see buffalo herds, they then make the sign of the cross and rush upon the buffalo at a gallop. This hunt is very dangerous and quite a few lost their lives when they fell off their horses or were trampled by the buffalo. But during the three months in which they had been praying to the true God, no accident had happened. This impressed them deeply and they explained to me: "Blackrobe, your prayer is powerful." Twice something happened, but it only strengthened the impression: One Indian had not gotten off his horse and prayed like the others when he saw the buffalo, but in his haste he had ridden ahead with the reins tangled. He was the only one who fell and the Indians ridiculed him.

Best at learning the prayer was a son of the chief at the age of about twelve years who had an extraordinary mind.[4] When the others gathered he was always first and spoke so loudly that everybody could follow him. I hope he will be one of my best assistants. Apart from him, I chose five of the best instructed to lead the prayers of the others during my absence. In the same way I chose three girls for the women. After good preparation they were all baptized in true belief and good faith. In heaven we have powerful intermediaries. I mean by this the children of this tribe who have died after having received the Sacrament of Baptism which washed away their sin. A month ago I baptized one of them and gave him the name Ignatius; a short time later he went to heaven. The Blackfeet have the custom of wrapping their dead in skins and covering them with branches, and occasionally one comes across these Indian graves. This time, however, they did not follow that custom but buried the child on the slope of a hill as I had recommended. In accordance with church custom we all went there and I said the prayers and set up the cross. The parents were consoled and said that they felt greatly strengthened by the sight of the cross.

[27]

Children's Baptisms among the Nonbelieving Indians

Saint Peter, June 12, 1876

P. C.

Dearest Parents,

A few days ago, upon returning from a trip to visit other Indians, I received your dear letter dated April 18.

This time there were about 250 lodges built together on the banks of the Badger River.[1] I spent the first few days in the lodge of the same chief I had stayed with last winter. Since I saw that everyone did remember all the prayers we had taught them, I went to stay with another chief, the first chief of the whole tribe called Little-feather. This poor Native deserves more compassion than the others because as a child he went to the mission at St. Ignatius where he was baptized and brought up Catholic, but then he returned to his tribe with all its ignorance and inbred licentiousness. Now he's a slave to four or five wives and I don't know if he'll ever want to leave them for eternal life in Heaven. He welcomed me warmly because he is fond of the Fathers and loves prayer; moreover, he is the most zealous promoter of baptism for the children. He sees prayer and baptism as the other Indians do: as nothing more than a way to have long life, perfect health, and plenty of hunting and worldly goods. You have all you can do to talk about and explain the spiritual effects of Baptism and of prayer, but almost all of them stop at this first step and it will take some time before they are able to move even a little bit beyond this. The chief I'm talking about, who, as I told you, was baptized as a child, is proof of the effectiveness of baptism as they see it, for he is the fattest of the whole nation. The first thing he told me last winter when he saw us was, "Look Blackrobe: I've been baptized," while patting his rotund belly! And if this isn't enough to make you pity them!

Nevertheless, for the time being we'll take what they give us. We teach them prayers and we baptize their children. It would be a lot worse if they believed, as has happened in the past, that prayer and baptism were medicines that cause the death of their children. Slowly but surely they will come to see things through faith and they'll discover all the wonders God grants us by way of the Sacraments and prayer.

I baptized another eighty-three children this time. An elderly Indian from the Kootenai tribe accompanied me around their native lodges in search of children not yet baptized.[2] The Kootenais, having already received adequate religious instruction, are exemplary and pious Catholics. This man of whom I'm speaking, who has been a great help to me, was led by Divine Providence to stay with the Blackfeet. Tirelessly, he went with me from lodge to lodge and spoke to everyone about baptism, just like an old catechist. In one lodge we encountered a man the Indians call a *Medicine man*, who are the most tenacious keepers of the Indian superstitions. Upon entering we asked him to have his children baptized. He answered no, saying that since he hadn't been baptized he wanted his children to be like him. I responded that baptism is for everyone and that even he could be baptized if first he left his wives and accepted the necessary instruction, but in the meantime he should ensure the eternal well being of his children. My speech was in vain and I was about to go when the elderly Kootenai said to me, "Wait, let me speak." Exactly what the good old man said is difficult for me to recount: it was all said in that dialect of theirs, with a reasoning and logic all its own, not to be found in any course of Eloquence, but which more than served its purpose. In any event, the Medicine man of the Blackfeet bowed his head and when the Kootenai had finished, he turned to me and said, "Baptize my children." I must confess I left the lodge a happy and wiser man. God had taught me a good lesson about my own limits and the strength of divine help and I said to myself: remember the fiasco of all your words and the effectiveness of the few words of the old Indian! The great chief gathered his people every evening to pray, so I was able to spend my time as best I could in preparing them to be converted.

While I was still at the camp, a party of about seventy Assiniboine Indians came from afar to make peace with the Blackfeet.[3] They were welcomed and everyone exchanged gifts, only to have to leave after a few days due to lack of food. In fact, the only thing to eat was a bit of jerky left over from the last hunt. This is why the Blackfeet didn't tarry in breaking camp to follow the buffalo. In summer the buffalo go North and the Natives travel as far as two hundred miles to hunt them again. The chiefs invited me to accompany them to the new camp but I couldn't accept this time because I had to spend the summer at the Mission where we're waiting for the Reverend Father Giorda to pay us a visit. The season has been very bad: cold and snow just as in winter. On the first of June snow fell several feet high and various horses died.

God has blessed me with good health in spite of difficulties, but when I'm amid these poor people I feel these deprivations only half as much as I should. May the Lord, despite my unworthiness, crown our efforts with the full conversion of this tribe.

Believe in me always
Your most devoted son
Philip S.J., Apostolic Missionary.

[28]

Apostolic Works at St. Peter's Mission

Mission of Saint Peter, March 11, 1877

P. C.

Dearest Parents,

I left for the Indian camp toward the end of October.[1] Almost all the Piegans (who are a tribe from the Blackfeet nation) were encamped along the Marias River at about one hundred miles from our residence. There were quite a number of Indians from other nations who had come from four hundred or more miles away to winter here and hunt buffalo.

I spent the first two weeks in the tepee of the same Chief who had welcomed me last winter. He remembered his prayers well and told me that he had continued to recite them every day. I even discovered that our faithful interpreter Baptiste had taught prayers to some of the other Indians during my absence. Therefore, I went to stay with another Chief of about fifty families. He suggested that I spend the rest of my time instructing this new part of our flock. I taught catechism morning and evening. At the sound of the bell the Blackfeet were the first to arrive, followed by others who spoke different languages, such as the Pend d' Oreilles and the Coeur d'Alenes, and who had been encamped close by for some time. These tribes are already Catholic and the Coeur d'Alenes were an especially great example and inspiration for the Blackfeet. I hope the Lord will finally move the heart of these poor infidels. Their greatest problem is polygamy. However, they don't balk at receiving instruction and they welcome our Lord even though they know that there are no halfway measures with His teachings. Indeed, this is no small feat toward receiving the grace of God.

I stayed with them all of January and throughout this time the Lord granted me good health and strength despite the fact that during the winter we ate and lived in their tepees as they did. Although I haven't done much yet, I am not dissatisfied with my efforts seeing that every time I go among them my presence is enough for them to receive sufficient grace for their conversion and that by doing this I am fulfilling the admirable provisions of Divine Providence for the salvation of all.

This time I baptized another hundred children. I received the confessions of about 150 natives, Pend d'Oreilles, Spokanes, and Coeur d'Alenes who were very pleased to have the blackrobe here so far from their own territory and to be able to partake of the Sacraments once again.[2] On Christmas Day I celebrated three Masses in a small house or perhaps I should say hut, made of beams and earth, which was the best we could find. Due to the close quarters of the site and the different languages, I had the Coeur d'Alenes come to the first Mass, the Spokanes and the Pend d'Oreilles to the second, and my poor Blackfeet to the third. As you know, during Mass all the Indians recite their prayers aloud and each tribe has its own devotional hymns. You can imagine my surprise at hearing the Coeur d'Alenes sing *adesto fideles*, in Latin, not to mention the others who sang the Kyrie, the Gloria, and so on just as the Whiteman would have done![3] This is due to the patience and the zeal of the Fathers who preceded us! And just what did the Blackfeet do at the third Mass? Why, these poor novices (if indeed they still deserve to be called this) recited their prayers and sang the principal points of the Catechism. Well, that's what we've achieved so far and I hope that the Christ Child will have accepted all of this and that He'll make this little seed grow. Of the Indian Catholics present, 135 participated in the Holy Communion.

While I remained here in this part of our Camp, Father Imoda was occupied in another part sixty miles from here. They are families of Métis, or descendents of Canadians married to Indians. The Oblate

Fathers were the first to take them under their wing and with admirable zeal and success were able to transform these families into a real Catholic community. These fifty families I'm telling you about now are but a small part of the other more numerous families that are presently scattered here and there living almost exclusively from hunting as the other Natives do. But the religious education they've received has taken such deep root that quite encouraging results can always be seen. Take, for example, these families encamped along the Milk River, who, in order to have a Father among them for a bit, sent two scouts all the way over here to our residence from 260 miles away. As soon as Father Imoda arrived at their encampment he was greatly pleased to see how eager they were to profit well from the Missionary's visit. There were more than 250 Holy Communions and everyone's faith and solid religious upbringing was amply demonstrated.

As best as their poverty allowed them, they too made an offering wholeheartedly to the Holy Father, which will be sent together with the others to celebrate the fiftieth anniversary of the Episcopal consecration of our beloved Pope. They even promised that on that day, the twenty-first of May, they'll recite the rosary for the Holy Father. We'll also have the Indians do the same so that all the languages and all the nations will be united in prayer for the Chief of the faithful.

I hope that these few lines will be well received by those who, as you tell me, take a special interest in our Missions. As you see, with this tribe we are still at the beginning. We would like to have a church and open a school for Indian children. It would cost at least eight to ten scudi per child per month, but at the moment we have all we can do just to support ourselves.[4] In short, we shall at least continue courageously to hope for what we can. Pray that the Lord bless and reward our work!

Your most affectionate son

Philip S.J., Apostolic Missionary.

[29]

On the Occasion of the Death of His Brother Luigi

Saint Peter, August 22, 1877[1]

P. C.

My dear Parents,

It's difficult for me to console you as I would like. I myself feel so overcome by this unexpected news that I don't know what to write; indeed, I only want to cry. However, to cry is not to console. When I think of Luigi and I think of you, I feel my heart breaking, which doesn't resolve anything.

The only consolation, the only comfort I have, is to uplift my heart and think of God, our Father! I still weep, but my weeping is unto the Lord. He willed this — this is the way it is and it is for the best because it is God's will. He has taken our and His beloved Luigi, not to tear him away from us, but to call him unto Himself. He took him because he loved him. He took him in the prime of his life, in the vigor of his youth, indeed in the best part of his life, because here on earth there is no youth, strength, or lasting joy so He gave it to him in eternity in Heaven. He took him at such a difficult time that we who remain will soon envy those who went before us. He took him unexpectedly, yet not entirely so, because how many times have we already put ourselves in His hands and let His will be done.

So be brave Father and Mother, sisters, brothers, and relatives: especially you, Ersilia, do not refuse the one true comfort we can have, compliance with divine will, however much it may cost our poor little hearts. God has been good to us so let us not refuse the crosses he sends. To bear a cross is an honor because it comes from God. He requires it of those whom he loves; He gives and takes earthly possessions in order to raise our hearts toward Heavenly riches.

I fervently pray for you and me. I pray that He help us and give us strength in facing this and other trials that He may send before uniting us forever.

Comfort me soon by telling me that you are trying to be strong! This is all I desire!

I leave you in the sacred Hearts of Jesus and Mary, our refuge and comfort.

Your most devoted son

Philip S.J., Apostolic Missionary.

[30]

The Encampment of the Métis

Saint Peter, September 19, 1877

P. C.

Reverend and Dearest Father Zampieri,

Thank you my dearest Father. I was already sure that you would not have failed to help me at this time. I see that you have also understood the thoughts that were afflicting me the most and I now feel that, as Mother and Father are overcoming their grief, I am, to a great extent, consoled.

I didn't respond immediately to your letter of the month of April, because shortly after I received it, I left to be among the Natives and I remained there nearly all summer long.

After returning here, I got the sad news of Luigi's death in a letter from my uncle. I immediately wrote home to console everyone as best I could, even though I myself needed consoling. Now I want to thank you and the other Fathers for all that has been done for my family in my stead. But more than anyone else I thank the Lord who knew, through His grave, how to help us shoulder the cross that He sent us to bear. It is useless for me to tell you for how many people in our family this loss is painful, but God, who knows this and loves us, wouldn't have allowed it to happen, if this too hadn't been in some way for our benefit. Therefore we must all comply with the will of the Lord and wholeheartedly make the sacrifice He requires of us.

Even what you tell me about Stanislao consoles me and encourages me quite a bit. I pray that God may give him the strength to look only for what He desires.

Now, I would like to give you some news about the Mission. . . .
First of all, the Indians I visited were not full-bloods, but Métis, that is, of mixed-blood. Moreover, they were not pagans, but practicing Catholics, converted by the zeal of the first Missionaries. Nonetheless, except for that, they live as Indians do, that is they roam around the plains with their tepees and families, following the buffalo herds upon which their survival is dependent. Their first Missionaries, the Oblate Fathers of the Immaculate Virgin and some secular Priests, succeeded in forming these nomadic families into sorts of villages with a stable Mission, Church, and schools. However, the nature of the Métis, although similar in many ways to that of the whiteman, takes not a little after that of the Indians with their lack of determination in the face of difficulties and their aversion to work. Indeed, in many of them, their Indian nature has won out and so, despite much work and hope on our part, they have taken to their tepees again and now survive as before from the hunt, which they conduct together in nomadic caravans of several families. Quite a few of these have come all the way to Blackfeet territory and now they too belong to our Mission. Despite the life they lead among tribes not converted and near Whitemen of unsavory lifestyles and no religion, the Métis generally remain constant in their love and practice of the faith they have received, as you will see in the following example. Since last winter they had been asking Father Imoda (who had visited and stayed with them awhile) that one of the Fathers return with them for the summer. This was not merely a whim, for at the beginning of June we saw two of them arrive on horseback to find the Father they had requested the previous winter and take him back. These two scouts had ridden for more than two hundred miles to get a Missionary. Father Guidi, however, had left for Bufford on the Missouri a few days earlier, to assist the soldiers there, and Father Imoda had to go to Helena.[1] As for me, I had already promised the Blackfeet Chiefs that this summer I would accompany the caravans of the Piegan Indians who are a part of that tribe. Nonetheless, we didn't have the heart to send them back with a negative reply after they had traveled so far. So Father Imoda decided that I

should first go with the caravans of the Métis, and if I should happen to discover the whereabouts of the Piegan encampment, then I would spend some time with them as well, so as to accommodate both their requests. So I left with the two scouts, and after riding for six days across the deserted plains we were within sight of the camp. On the other side of the Milk River there were forty-two tepees or families who were about to break camp because the Buffalo herds had gone away. They had only been waiting for me. The warm manner in which they greeted me is without compare. The morning of the sixth day, when they had foreseen I would arrive, about forty men on horseback came out to meet me fifteen miles from camp. What surprised me the most was that as they approached me they divided into two rows, dismounted, and on their knees fired rifle shots into the air.[2] Then they asked me to bless them, and after shaking my hand, remounted and accompanied me to the tepees. There I found women, children, and the elderly all gathered on top of a hill. All of them too knelt down, asking me to bless them, and then came to shake my hand. Since they didn't know whether or not I had brought a tepee, they had readied one of theirs for me, supplied with the best everyone had to offer. They even brought me their choicest game and some provisions, such as rice, flour, etc., that they had bought from the Whitemen by selling furs. I had, however, brought my own tipi and some provisions for the journey. When leaving from the Rectory it's just about impossible to take all the provisions one needs for the entire time spent at the Camps (especially when you have to stay a long time). We generally manage by making do with what is available and forge ahead. The Métis do a lot more for the Fathers than the other Natives. Sometimes there is also the possibility of buying something from the Whitemen who come to trade furs, other times (when nothing else is available) one relies on the hunt. When there is nothing to hunt, Natives and Missionaries alike rely on packs of jerky and no one starves. The day after I arrived we moved camp in search of Buffalo. After traveling for two days we were fortunate enough to see Buffalo herds grazing on the plains in the distance. So as soon as they found water, the families set up the tepees and the following day each of the hunters returned with a fresh supply of meat. In short, this is what happened for the first days and is what happens during the whole year, so I won't bother repeating it because, as I've said before, this is how these people live year round and are indeed content with living their whole lives this way.

However, I will tell you about my part in the Holy Ministry, and what it is like in our roving parish, especially since this time I'm among Catholics.

Every morning I celebrated Holy Mass at around seven, except when it rained which was only three times. Our bell, a large shell, was loud enough to be heard from a distance. When it rang everyone quickly left their tepees and came to the altar: a prairie altar which was adorned with the best they had, but most of all, with their religious fervor. When the Mass was sung, since they had been instructed so well by the first Missionaries, they sang the Kyrie, Glory to God, the Creed, etc., just as well as we do at our Parishes. Several of them can read and write not only in French and English, but in their Native Cree or Sautaux as well. Those who lead the singing held the book (the Graduale Romanum) reading the Latin words and musical notes very well.[3] You can see by this what the zeal of those first Fathers was able to accomplish among these poor people, and how much more they could accomplish if only they abandoned their nomadic way of living once again.

I preached twice a day, once after the Gospel, and again after the evening prayers. Around nine in the morning and three in the afternoon I taught Catechism to the children. So twice a day I taught them to read. In the evening everyone recited the Rosary together and sang spiritual hymns.

The Chiefs always set aside enough time for these activities even when they moved camp and traveled. In fact, camp was never broken until after Mass. When traveling they stopped to rest the horses and themselves, and then Catechism and instruction for the children took place before moving on. Since traveling on the plains takes place in an orderly fashion, a guide is nominated each time to lead the caravan and no one can go ahead of him. Each family follows, one behind the other in a long single file. The guide, at the head of the single file, carried a waving flag with a Cross emblazoned on it.

When it was time for the buffalo chase, it was beautiful to see all those men on horseback gathered together on top of a hill, dismount, lay down their arms, and kneel in prayer, reciting an Our Father, Hail Mary, and an act of contrition. Then they all galloped off at breakneck speed to the extremely dangerous hunt. Throughout the entire summer, although several had fallen from their horses or had been exposed to the fury of wounded bulls, there weren't any serious accidents to speak of.

Traveling like this across the plains, we encountered on more than one occasion other caravans of Métis, all of whom were pleased to be able to listen to Mass and receive the Sacraments for a couple of days.

Among just the Métis this summer I baptized 21 newborn babies, received 250 confessions, celebrated 2 marriages and 220 communions.

As promised, toward the end of July I decided to visit the poor Blackfeet. We knew their tepees were far on the other side of the Cypress Mountains in English territory.[4] I took the opportunity of going along with some Métis who had to go in that direction and so at last I found myself once again among more than two hundred Piegan and Blood families. The chiefs welcomed me very warmly. I was pleased, not for myself but for our cause, to see these poor pagan Natives marveling and taking strength in the fact that the Blackrobe should, despite everything, join them in this wasteland. I remained with them for two weeks and baptized about one hundred babies.

That, dear Father, is all that I had to tell you. As you can see, with the Métis I reaped the fruit of what others had sown and now, among the pagan Blackfeet, am merely preparing the way. Indeed this is exactly what does encourage me: that only the fruit of seeds which have been sown can be reaped and that well-prepared terrain, with God's help and our own efforts will, in time, bear fruit, *fructum afferet in patientia* [patience will bear fruit].

I sincerely ask you and whoever believes in our mission to remember me in your prayers.

In union with Holy Saints have faith in me always.

Your most affectionate in Jesus Christ

Philip Rappagliosi S.J., Apostolic Missionary.

[31]

On the Occasion of the Death of His Other Brother, Stanislao

Benton, October 14, 1877

P. C.

Dearest Parents,

The good Father Zampieri, who did so much for Stanislao and the rest of you, came to console me as well. I say console because indeed the things he writes about our dear deceased are such that the Lord must be praised, even while we feel the pain of this new loss.[1] I was prepared for the news when it reached me, so it was less painful to me than the news of poor Luigi. Here, too, let the will of God be done.

The Lord has taken two loved ones from us in such a short time, but remember that they were taken away from us to give them back to us eternally. I feel your pain more than others, but I hope that God's comfort is in direct proportion to the trial He has set for you. Therefore take heart; be calm and surrender to the Lord with all your being.

These past months, oh! what months they have been for you! I can see it as if I had seen you every day. But those months are also your crowning glory, as times of trial and tribulation are the most valuable before God.

Luigi and Stanislao, now united in heaven, do not forsake us, whom you so loved on earth and by whom you were so loved! . . .

Even though I traveled day and night to get here in time, I only just arrived yesterday. There was a battle between the soldiers and some of the Nez Perce rebels.[2] The soldiers had twenty-two dead and forty wounded; the Natives seventeen dead and I don't know how many wounded. The battle took place a hundred miles from here. Father Imoda immediately sent me to take care of the wounded, but before I arrived they had been taken down the Missouri on boats.

Land that the Natives don't want to hand over to the Whites is the reason for this war. It's always the same story, a very shameful one indeed for the Whites who make treaties and then violate them. Now it seems that everything is at an end. Three hundred fifty Nez Perces, including children and women, have surrendered; a few others have fled. The other tribes are quiet.

I'll stay here for next Sunday's Mass, then I'll return to the Mission. After that, I'll return again to the Blackfeet camp.

Farewell Father, Mother, Sister, and brothers. Farewell to all of you and have faith in God. Pray for me always and for these poor Natives. I embrace you with all my heart.

Your most affectionate son
Philip S.J., Apostolic Missionary.

[32]
Words of Comfort to His Relatives
Saint Peter, November 15, 1877
P. C.

Dearest Parents and Relatives,

I was given your letter dated September the twenty-sixth on the third of this month. It arrived here on the twenty-ninth of October but on that day I was still on assignment.

As I see, and as it was natural, you unburden yourself a little with me. The things you tell me, trouble me on the one hand, because they are true and there is no human remedy for them; however, on the other hand I am glad that you tell me, because if you cannot unburden yourselves freely with me, with whom else can you do it? But take heart, my dear ones. The Lord knows the situation you are in and the proof he wants from you. For goodness sake, don't hesitate to go to Him and to weep at His feet if you want real solace. I know that you do that already, which is what comforts me the most because no one on earth can fully console us.

As for myself, I am by your side and close to you in spirit. I must say that I know how much you have suffered and are still suffering. It's as though I can see it with my own eyes; but aside from praying to God, which indeed I believe is the best thing to do, I can't do much else.

So take heart, Father, Mother, Sister, and brothers.

I am consoled quite a bit to see from Father and Mother's letter that the Lord is in fact your guide and that the feelings of faith and Christian obedience accompany you even as you express the pain you feel. This is what the Lord wants from you.

After receiving your last letter, I had to go here and there to visit families scattered about, celebrating the holy Mass first in one house, then in another. I was on the road for several days and returned home yesterday. I shall return shortly to the Indian Camp and by the time this letter reaches you, I shall be among them once again.

I will always pray for you and offer unto God, also for you, my small sufferings at the Camp, and I will suffer especially in the winter, as I have already described. You, too, pray for me and the poor Indians.

Our last two dear deceased are always on my mind, especially when I am at the holy altar. I have already celebrated several Masses for them and other Fathers have done the same. I feel in my heart that they are already better off than we are, and that they are praying for us, the people whom they loved down here. What more can we desire? . . .

I am in good health and the Lord has given me strength thus far. Let's proceed with courage.

Father Imoda sends his greetings and remembers you in his prayers.

I don't have anything else to tell you for now. I'll write you from the Indian Camp as soon as I can.

Farewell, I embrace you with all my heart. Console yourselves as much as you can for my sake.

Your most affectionate son
Philip S.J., Apostolic Missionary.

[33]

Departure for the Last Mission

Benton, January 1, 1878

P. C.

Dearest Brother,

I received your letter yesterday upon my arrival here in Benton. Thank you for the New Year's wishes which I return to all, a hundredfold.

Last month I was with 108 Métis families who are spending this winter along the Milk River. I returned to Benton to see Father Imoda who was expected to come today, on the first of the year. In fact, I had the pleasure of meeting him as planned and I shall return shortly to the Milk River camp. Father Imoda has asked me to remain there for another month and then travel on to the Blackfeet, whom I've not yet seen this winter.

Praise the Lord, I'm in good health.

God willing, when I finish this trip, I'll send a brief account as I've done in the past.[1]

I have learned with pleasure in a letter from dear Brother Lattanzi that he is coming soon to the Rocky Mountains. Praise be to God for the new help that He is sending us and blessed be he who comes in the name of God.

I celebrated Midnight Mass at Christmas and everyone at the camp participated with much religious fervor; however, I'll write more about this later.

Now I'm only passing through and have very little time. I'm just sending these few lines so that you all know how I am and continue to pray for me and this Mission.

Remain courageous, my dear ones, in the trial that God has sent you and for which He will give you abundant recompense.

Best wishes for the New Year, and especially strength and acceptance of the Lord's will. Please give my best to all the relatives.

Thank Mother and Father for the kind words they appended to your letter. . . .

Farewell, dear brother, I embrace you with all my heart.

Your most affectionate brother

Philip S.J., Apostolic Missionary.

Obituary

Father Philip Rappagliosi in Montana, 1873–78, by Joseph Guidi, S.J.

In the autumn of 1873, Fr. Rappagliosi bade adieu to Europe, and, after a long and fatiguing voyage arrived at the Rocky Mountains on the twenty-first of December of the same year. Having taken some necessary rest at our residence of Helena, which is the first one meets on coming to our mission, he proceeded to St. Mary's among the Flatheads about 170 miles farther west. This was, for the present, the field appointed for his apostolic labors. The object of his ardent desires was now attained. He was in the midst of the poor Indians in whose service he was willing to spend himself, and even to lay down his life, that he might win their souls to God. He at once set himself down to learn their language, with the docility of a child and the earnestness of an apostle. When he had mastered a few phrases he would go among the Indians to repeat them. In this way, and by noting down the most common words which he afterward committed to his faithful memory, he was soon able to make himself understood. He noticed also, that the Indians make great use of gestures in conversation; and of this fact he availed himself to make them more readily comprehend what he said.[1] These poor people soon perceived the love of the good Father for them and readily yielded to his affectionate exhortations. Whenever a new lodge settled in the vicinity of the mission he set out to visit it, taking with him some pious images which he distributed among those whose influence was more powerful for good. If the newcomers had for some time neglected their Christian duties, his zeal gave him no rest till by exhortation and entreaty he had recalled them to the observance of God's holy law. There lived among the Flatheads some families of the Nez Perces who were yet infidels. These he visited frequently, taught them their prayers, gave them some rudimentary instruction, and hoped soon to add them to the fold of Christ; but he was called away by holy obedience and sent to the mission of St. Ignatius, sixty-five miles to the north, among the Pend d'Oreilles, who are allied to the Flatheads and have the same language, customs, and faith. He soon endeared himself to his new flock so that they sought him in all their troubles and followed his instructions with docility. A Father who was his companion at the mission of St. Ignatius, writes of him as follows: "The good Fr. Rappagliosi is a source of edification to us all. He has the charity of an apostle, and labors unceasingly for the poor Indians."[2]

Fr. Rappagliosi was not allowed to remain long here; and yet he so won the hearts of all, that, when he was removed, the chief of the tribe came to ask the superior of the mission to send back the black-gown who was so much beloved by his people.[3] One day when he had returned from a missionary excursion, his heart filled with sorrow for the destitution and misery both temporal and spiritual, that he had seen, he said to me with enthusiasm: "Oh! that I had the means to alleviate the distress I witness around me." He did not spare himself in doing what he could for his Indians; he spoke to them words of comfort, he instructed them; he exhorted them to peace and to the practice of Christian virtue; he set them the example of bearing hardship without repining. Like a veteran missionary, he adapted himself to their mode of living; no self-denial was too great, provided he could gain souls to Christ. The Lord was pleased with his holy desires and labors, and called him early to his reward.

Toward the summer of 1875, the mission of St. Peter was opened among the Blackfeet. These savages have been hostile, and they are so corrupted by the wicked conduct of the whites who have come among them, that the fatigue and labor of the missionary are repaid with but little fruit. In fact, very few respond to our exhortations; almost all being sunk in brutal polygamy. Still, in spite of such general depravity, there is some good to be gleaned, and the heart of the patient missionary is gladdened when he is allowed to baptize the infants, which die in great numbers from want of proper care and nourishment. In the hope of working a change for the better in this tribe, the superior general of the mission sent Fr. Rappagliosi thither. But here he was met by a new difficulty; the dialect spoken [by the Blackfeet was different from that spoken] by the Nez Perces and Pend d'Oreilles, so that he had to begin over again the arduous task of learning a new and difficult language. God's greater glory and the salvation of souls required it, and, however painful the work, he was ready to undertake it at whatever cost. During some months, he might be seen daily going to a family of half-breeds, who lived about a mile from the mission, to practice some phrases which he had learned and to pick up a few words more to add to his vocabu-lary.[4] Another difficulty was, that the Blackfeet lead a roving life, remaining no more than two or three weeks in one place. Moreover, the whites had encroached on their hunting grounds N. E. of the mission, and the bison having withdrawn farther to the north, the Indians were obliged to follow them, so that the principal camp-ing grounds were thus removed about one hundred miles from the mission. This is a great inconvenience and exposes the missionary to many hardships; for the route lies across a desert prairie exposed in summer to the hot parching rays of the sun, and to the piercing north winds in winter.

In December 1876, Fr. Rappagliosi took charge of his new field of evangelical labor, and remained in the Indian encampment during several months. There is no describing the privations he suffered during this time; for as yet his knowledge of the language spoken by the Blackfeet was very imperfect, and it was with difficulty he could convey his meaning by the aid of gestures. Add to this, the monotony of savage life, the food, and the annoying insects which swarm in the Indian lodges. He spent the time chiefly in mastering the language and in teaching the children their prayers. On Sundays he said Mass in a neighboring store owned by an enterprising white. Here with the aid of an interpreter, he gave instructions to the few Indians who attended, and insisted on the necessity of having their children baptized. His efforts in this respect were fairly successful, and about one hundred received the Sacrament of Baptism during his stay among them. He departed from the Indian camp late in the spring, and came to the mission to enjoy a brief repose. Then the zealous missionary set out to visit the whites, sparsely scattered over the Territory. His sweet and affable manners were sufficient recommendations to gain the goodwill and attention of those who, differing from him in faith, were inclined to show little respect for his sacred ministry. He advanced rapidly in their esteem; but his heart was with the poor unfriended Indians. "It is, indeed, difficult to convert the old; but, with care and attention, the young may be made good Christians. If I had an orphanage under the management of the sisters of Charity," he used to say; "I would soon have the Blackfeet completely changed. The children would be educated in a pious, Christian manner of life, and they, by their prayers and influence, would then convert their parents. But the mission is too poor to bear the expenses of such an undertaking, and the unfortunate Indians must go to destruction. Ah! that some generous benefactor would come to my assistance."

Many and beautiful were the virtues which he practiced toward his brethren in religion. Like every true son of the Society of Jesus, he was all sweetness and charity. His conversation was pleasant, mingled with Roman wit, but without bitterness; a harsh word or cutting remark never passed his lips. He spoke and thought well of every one of his brethren, and deemed himself most happy when he could render them the least service. When they would return from their missionary excursions, he used to unsaddle their horses and put them in the stable, and then he would do all in his power to procure for the Father a speedy rest. His esteem for obedience made him seek its sanction in the smallest actions. He always asked his superiors for advice, both before setting out on his excursions, and when absent on the field of labor. "I will do what I can," he would say, when speaking of this virtue, "but above all, I long to have the blessing of obedience on my undertakings. May God grant me the grace to die, rather than I should act independently of our superiors."

It was thus Fr. Rappagliosi prepared himself for the heroic labors and sacrifices of the mission of the Blackfeet Indians, which was soon afterward assigned to him. While on this mission, necessity often forced him to travel many miles over vast and dreary prairies without a guide or companion, and with the few provisions one horse could carry. Stores of provisions were established along the encampments of the Indians, and money was furnished him by superiors for necessary supplies; but it not seldom happened, that his little stock of food gave out on account of the length of the journey, or the rainy weather, which rendered traveling almost impossible.[5] On such occasions he had often to be satisfied with buffalo meat cooked after the manner of the Indians.

The spring of the year 1877 was destined by Providence to be a time of great toil and sacrifice for Fr. Rappagliosi. He betook himself to the camp of the Indians, and found that provisions had given out and that the Indians were devoid of all means of subsistence.[6] The wretched Blackfeet in order to satisfy the cravings of hunger were forced to go in search of dead buffalo which had been killed during the preceding winter. He told me confidently afterward, that during his stay among them, he often suffered from extreme hunger. A few days after his return from the camp of the Blackfeet, a courier from the Milk River arrived at the mission, having traveled a distance of two hundred miles to announce that the presence of a Father was desired by many Christian families of the Métis, who had settled in the neighborhood of the Milk River for the purpose of buffalo hunting. Two of the three Fathers were then occupied in the ministry, and it fell to the lot of Fr. Rappagliosi to visit the Métis. He made use of this opportunity to visit another camp of the Blackfeet, situated many miles farther north. In an account of this excursion which he gave to his superior, he says: "These good Métis gave me a reception fit for a pope. They sent a covered carriage to Fort Belknap for my conveyance.[7] Ten miles from the camp, forty horsemen met me, separated into two columns and fired their guns. On the rising slope, above which they had pitched their camp, the old men, women, and children stood in groups waiting for my approach, extending their hands toward me as I drew near. I hope that these good dispositions toward the minister of God will induce them to take advantage of this opportunity." Soon, however, matters underwent a change for the worse. He thus writes to his superior: "My health is good, but our provisions are so reduced that meat alone, and often only dry meat forms our scanty meal. The Indians cannot buy me anything, for there are no stores along the Milk River. Mosquitoes and vermin are in abundance, and frequently our wigwams are overturned by the storm. To be drenched with rain for hours is not uncommon with me; yet blessed by the good God, I feel no effects such as rheumatism, colds, etc., though, as you know, my constitution is not of the strongest." From the camp of the Métis he set out on a long and wearisome journey to visit some Blackfeet encamped many miles beyond the boundary of the United States, in the British Possessions. God rewarded his zeal with the baptism of about one hundred infants.

On the nineteenth of August he returned to our mission station, much emaciated and worn out with fatigue. At other times when returning from his excursions he would recover his lost strength after a few days' rest. But this time his recovery was slow. He often said, that he felt very weak and fatigued; notwithstanding all this he kept up his courage, and thought of nothing but of winning to God the poor, abandoned Blackfeet. I remember having often advised him not to expose his health so much, but to take a little care of it, especially, since the Blackfeet did not show themselves as yet disposed for conversion, on account of polygamy, which, as has been already remarked, is prevalent among them, and is, under existing circumstances, most difficult to be abolished. But he would reply: "Someone must expose and even lose his life for the establishment of the mission."

Toward the end of September, I was removed from the Blackfeet mission, on the score of ill health, and then only two Fathers were left to cultivate that vast and thorny field. It was a task beyond their strength; but the scarcity of priests did not allow the superior general to reinforce them. About the middle of November Fr. Rappagliosi put himself in readiness to visit the camps of the Blackfeet along the river Marias, when, from the camp of the Métis, which he had visited last summer, a messenger arrived asking for a priest to assist a dying woman. Fr. Rappagliosi had to undertake the journey. Strange, as it seemed, he embraced all before departing, and in taking leave of Fr. Negro spoke these mysterious words: "Dear brother, should I return no more, pray for the peace of my soul." On the twenty-eighth of Nov. he arrived in the camp of the Métis; but a sad spectacle presented itself to his eyes. The wily enemy of salvation had walked through that hopeful field and sowed the cockle. Many of those who had before shown such excellent dispositions, having been ill advised and wrongly informed of his good intentions, now shunned him, and even went so far as to insult him. This unexpected treatment inflicted a deep wound on his tender heart. In a letter to one of the Fathers he says that he suffered an eight days' martyrdom. He endeavored notwithstanding to work for the salvation of those who remained faithful and to prevent dissensions between the two parties. After Christmas, he went to Benton, a little town about halfway between Milk River and the mission-house, and there met Fr. Imoda, his superior, from whom he received orders to visit the Piegans up the Marias River.[8] Fr. Imoda on bidding him farewell, noticed that he looked somewhat pale, and thinking he was sick, told him to stay a short time to recruit his strength, or, if he felt really ill, to return to the mission-house, as he himself would take his place. But Fr. Rappagliosi replied in these words: "I do not feel any indisposition, dear Father, but it seems to me, nevertheless, that I go to die; still I must go." On the third of January Fr. Rappagliosi left Benton, and reached the camp of the Métis on the seventh, taking up his lodging in an old hut of but one apartment, owned by a certain Mr. Alexander Weekly. Scarcely had he arrived at the camp, when he began to feel indisposed. On the twentieth of January, which fell on Sunday, he said Mass and preached, though he was not well. In the afternoon he rode to another camp some miles off, here he was taken ill again, and this time rather seriously. He sent at once for Mr. Weekly, who, on receiving his message, made no delay in coming. Judging from the symptoms that the illness would be of a serious nature, he helped the Father into a carriage and brought him back to his own house. While there, Fr. Rappagliosi wrote two letters, one to his superior, who was at a distance of two hundred miles; the other to Fr. de Courby, an Oblate residing twenty miles north of the Milk River. The letter to Fr. Imoda was entrusted to an American on his way to Benton; the other was sent by a special messenger. The Métis wished to call a doctor, but Fr. Rappagliosi advised them not to do so, saying that a physician could be of no assistance to him since his disease was situated principally in the heart.[9] On January the twenty-second he had a violent attack of fever which deprived him of the use of his senses. On the twenty-third he was again well and talked freely. He asked Mr. Weekly, who had a board in his hand, whether he was going to make a coffin. On the same day a Mr. Brooks visited the Father, and was requested by him to hasten to Fort Belknap and get possession of the letter to Fr. Imoda, which had been given to the American traveler. He set out at once, succeeded in getting the letter, and returned it to Fr. Rappagliosi, who, thinking that he had exaggerated the account of his sickness, tore it up. On the following night he grew worse. His senses failed him, and his mind began to wander. Toward midnight the fever became less violent, and he recovered the use of his senses. Mrs. Weekly, who had nursed him with the tenderness of a mother, offered him some nourishment. He accepted it, thanking her for her great kindness and solicitude. The Métis also, it must be said, endeavored by every possible means to bring relief to the Father; buying for him the best things in the store at Fort Belknap.

"Tell the Fathers," said the sick man to Mrs. Weekly, "that the cause of my sickness is chiefly in the heart, and that in my opinion, my grief, rather than my malady will bring about my death; but I deem it a signal favor of God to allow me to die here and in the midst of you." Next morning he requested her to call in all the children, because, he said, he wished to recommend himself to their prayers. Then he exclaimed: "My heart rejoices at the thought, that I am to die among you. I love you all tenderly, because you are my spiritual children; and I have made an offering to God of my life for your welfare." When his hostess, Mrs. Weekly, told him that his death would leave them deprived of all spiritual assistance, and that in those lonely regions it was not, as in Europe, where the post left vacant by the death of priest, is quickly filled by another, he replied, that he was glad to end his days among them, because it was God's most holy will.

On the twenty-fourth of January Fr. de Courby arrived. Fr. Rappagliosi was then in full possession of his senses, made his confession, and received holy Communion. After Communion he again lost the use of his senses, and with the exception of a few lucid moments remained in this state until death. During these short intervals of consciousness he would call the children around his bed and make them pray. As long as Fr. Rappagliosi was ill, Mr. Weekly, in order not to be a source of annoyance to the sick man, lived in a tent hard by. When the Father heard of it, he thanked Mr. Weekly very much for his great kindness. Meanwhile Mr. Brooks attended the missionary with the utmost care, as if he had been his own son. On the fourth of February Fr. de Courby gave Fr. Rappagliosi Extreme Unction, and then left him, having been called away by pressing duties. After his departure Fr. Rappagliosi sank rapidly. Those who attended him, thinking his end was near, summoned around his bed a great number of Métis, who, falling on their knees, prayed most fervently for his happy passage to eternity.[10] Thus amid the prayers and tears of these good Christians, Fr. Rappagliosi gave up his soul to his Creator, on the seventh of February at 7:30 o'clock P.M.

Fr. Rappagliosi's remains were placed in a metal coffin, and brought to Benton. Fr. Imoda arrived the same day, and on the following morning he said a Mass of Requiem, at which many Catholics assisted. The corpse was then conveyed to the mission of St. Peter where another Mass was said, and thence to Helena. At Helena many Catholics of the city went out with hearse and carriages to meet the stagecoach thinking that it would bring the body. But it came by wagon, and arrived much later. After High Mass on Sunday, the seventeenth, it was carried in procession through the church, and after the last rites had been performed over it, and an appropriate funeral address delivered, it was laid to rest in the vault under the sacristy.[11]

Fr. Rappagliosi sleeps in the peace of the Lord, and his memory is held in benediction. Protestants as well as Catholics speak of him as of an apostle and saint. The poor Indians, who always found in him a true friend, a kind benefactor, and a tender father, especially grieved over his death. On hearing of it, they were inconsolable and prayed with many tears for his soul. At the missions of St. Mary and St. Ignatius, solemn Mass was sung, at which many went to Communion. The Coeur d'Alenes, who knew the Father only by report, received the news of his death with mourning, and the chief of their tribe offered the superior of that mission money for celebrating a solemn Mass of Requiem. The superior refused the money, but celebrated the Mass, at which the Indians sang and many communicated. Some of the Flatheads and Pend d'Oreilles, in passing through Helena, asked to see the grave of the Father, and when at the place, prayed on their knees most devoutly. God seems to have required the life of the Father as a pledge for the success of the mission. His end is worthy of a true son of the Society, for he fell with honor on the field of his labors. — R. I. P.

Questions Surrounding Rappagliosi's Death

Philip Rappagliosi's letters and Joseph Guidi's biographical sketch are frustratingly vague about the conflict between Father Jean Baptiste Marie Genin, O.M.I., and Rappagliosi in the Milk River Métis camps during the winter of 1877–78. The surviving documents do not even explain what the competition was about. There is also no way to tell what part the contest played in Rappagliosi's death. Some new evidence surrounding the conflict and death of Rappagliosi has been located, but many questions are still unanswered.

Father Guidi's biography suggests that Rappagliosi's health was frail before 1878, but Guidi did not actually describe the health problems Rappagliosi had before coming to the Rocky Mountains. In his 1856 letter to his parents requesting their permission to join the Society of Jesus, Rappagliosi said obliquely that he believed his health could adapt to the life of a novice because "I have recovered considerably." He did not say from what he had recovered. Rappagliosi did seem to go out of his way in the letters to frequently assure his parents that he was in good health. Father Guidi reported that while at St. Peter's Mission, Rappagliosi mentioned to his superior that "my constitution is not of the strongest." None of the sources located, however, explain why Rappagliosi died that winter when so many other missionaries, Métis, and Indians in the same camps survived.

The two pictures of Rappagliosi in the Oregon Province Archives of the Society of Jesus in Spokane, Washington, may indicate a general deterioration of his health while he was in Montana. The picture used as a frontispiece for the 1879 edition of the Memorie was taken by M. A. Eckert, a photographer in Helena in the 1870s. In this picture Rappagliosi appears frail but healthy. The picture of Rappagliosi that appeared in the 1894 edition of Indian and White in the Northwest, by Father Lawrence B. Palladino, S.J., was taken by O. C. Bundy, a photographer at Virginia City, Montana Territory, during the 1870s. The Bundy picture shows Rappagliosi with sunken eyes and sallow skin. Neither picture can be dated precisely, but if the Bundy picture was taken later than the Eckert picture, it would suggest that Rappagliosi's health was in decline even before his last visit to the Métis camp in 1878.[1]

Guidi's description of the events surrounding Rappagliosi's death was quite vague in the obituary in *Woodstock Letters* (reprinted in appendix A). During the winter of 1877–78, while Father Rappagliosi was at the Métis camp on the Milk River, Father Genin was staying in a neighboring Métis camp. Genin and Rappagliosi competed for the allegiance of the Métis. Father Camillo Imoda, S.J., the superior of St. Peter's Mission, wrote on March 4, 1878, that in November 1877 Genin

was causing an uproar in that [Métis] camp formenting dissension and causing much scandal. Father Rappagliosi informed me of the state of affairs, and he tried as best he could to fix those problems. . . . Father Genin had turned some of the Métis against the Father [Rappagliosi], and when he returned he was received coldly, and some approached him with some insulting objections. These things had such an effect on the sensitive nature of Father Philip that he came down with a fever that dispatched him in about twenty days. One shouldn't think that all the Métis were against Father Rappagliosi, it was only a few that took sides against him, many were indifferent, and others, mainly the elders and the chiefs, were on his [Rappagliosi's] side, so that fights ensued between the two sides, that Father Philip tried to stave off.[2]

In *Indian and White in the Northwest*, Palladino recorded that "the last letter written by Father Rappagliosi was addressed to us [me]. It was written in pencil some eight days before his death. In that letter, after alluding to some of his trials, the heart-broken missionary asked, as a matter of conscience, that the Ordinary who had jurisdiction over that part of the country might be made acquainted with the religious state of affairs thereabout, a lamentable state, which entailed the ruin of souls, and was hastening the Father to his grave. We [I] complied with his dying request, transmitting his letter to the proper authorities."[3] Genin wrote two letters about the events of that winter on the Milk River, both published in the *New York Freeman's Journal*. The first was dated December 13, 1877, and told about the "treacherous machinations of one white man" who incited some unnamed Indians to attempt to kill Genin. Genin survived, but his letter suggests that the attempted assassination occurred before he made a trip to Sitting Bull's camp in August 1877. His next letter, dated September 5, 1878, describes his residence among the Métis on the Milk River during the winter of 1877-1878 but makes no mention of Rappagliosi or any conflict with another priest. Genin does claim that his warm reception among the Sioux and Métis and his "perfect liberty and safety in his movements among the Indians, created grave suspicions, I might say, serious jealousy in military and other quarters. Three spies, headed by a large, soulless, body, were paid at the rate of $100 a week to watch me, and the checks for the payment of their important work were issued somewhere at Fort Keogh, on the Yellowstone River." Whether there might be a connection between the military spies and Rappagliosi's death is unknown.[4] In sum, the available sources make vague references to conflict between Rappagliosi and Genin during the winter of 1877-78, but they do not indicate what the conflict was about.

Father Genin (1837-1900) had been ordained in the Oblates of Mary Immaculate in 1864 and was appointed as a missionary to the Indians of the Northern Plains the following year. During the next twelve years he worked primarily among the Métis, Sioux, and Chippewas in Canada and the United States. Genin was adopted as a brother by Sitting Bull and respected by those Sioux who were hostile to the U.S. government in the 1870s.[5]

In 1876 Genin was expelled from the Oblate congregation, but the materials in the Oblate Archives in Rome fail to explain the specific reasons for the expulsion. He was charged with violating his vows of poverty, chastity, and obedience, but no specific incidents were mentioned. Genin denied the charges in November 1876, saying that his only violation of the vow of poverty was to send some small support to his parents without formal permission. He categorically denied any violation of his vow of chastity. The accusations regarding obedience, Genin claimed, resulted from an order to appear in Ottawa, fifteen hundred miles from his station in Duluth, Minnesota, when he did not have the funds to make such a trip. After his expulsion he spent twenty-four more years among the Métis, Indians, and whites of the Northern Plains as a secular priest and was responsible for starting a number of Catholic churches for white immigrants in the Dakotas. According to Gaston Carrière's *Dictionnaire biographique des Oblats de Marie-Immaculée au Canada*, Genin had numerous bitter quarrels with his bishop in the early 1880s, so his troubles with church authorities continued.[6]

In the winter of 1877–78 the U.S. Army and the Indian Service accused Genin of trading ammunition with the Métis and hostile Sioux. Sitting Bull's band were living as refugees in Canada at this time, and Métis and Indians, both hostile and friendly to the United States, were being drawn to the Milk River by the rapidly shrinking buffalo herds. The U.S. Army tried to prevent all of the buffalo-hunting tribes from buying ammunition and guns in order to weaken the firepower of the hostiles.

Father Genin argued that the buffalo robes he obtained during the winter of 1877–78 were an offering from his Métis congregation, not the proceeds from trade. According to Genin, Sitting Bull's camp had a good supply of ammunition and arms captured from the U.S. Army, and the Sioux were able to refill their cartridges. The Métis in Father Genin's camp had "never yet furnished them any cartridges, as some people have thought and said."[7]

Genin did admit to feeding and doctoring Nez Perce refugees from the Battle of the Bear Paws in 1877 as a humanitarian gesture. In a December 13, 1877, letter, Genin explained: "How could a priest refuse his attention to suffering humanity? The good half-breeds fed those poor Indians, whilst I washed and wrapped their wounds. The Gros Ventre Indians treated differently those they happened to reach; they killed them, and were praised by the people of the United States, whilst the actions of the half-breeds and mine evoked a serious suspicion in army quarters. However, the cloud soon vanished, and the officers understood we could not reason, at such a juncture, upon the merits or demerits of that so unexpected war."[8] Many of the Nez Perce refugees then joined Sitting Bull's camp in Canada. In addition, Genin was publishing letters in the *New York Freeman's Journal* in which he gave the Indians' perspective on the Northern Plains battles of the 1870s and argued that white people were not racially superior to Indians. These radical ideas, combined with Father Genin's free travel among the hostile camps, were probably part of the reason the U.S. Army spied on him during this period.

This background, however, does not explain for sure what Genin and Rappagliosi fought about during that winter on the Milk River. Father Camillo Imoda, S.J., argued that Rappagliosi died of grief over the conflict and the loss of allegiance of the Métis.[9] Henry Brooks, a white man who nursed Rappagliosi during his last illness, assured Father Palladino that Rappagliosi did not want for food or care at the end. According to Brooks, Rappagliosi "was not in the best of health upon his first arrival" in November 1877. Brooks explained that he "had everything for him [Rappagliosi]. Can fruits, vegetables, best of bread and butter. There was nothing wanting for him in the way of food. I cooked it myself for him, baked the bread, and held him up in my arms like a child, when he was eating. The father was out of his mind (with rare intervals) for about 13 days before death." Brooks also accused Genin of causing Rappagliosi's death because "through word and deed [Genin] gave trouble to the poor father." Brooks reported that Genin gave Rappagliosi some unknown medicine a few days before Rappagliosi died.[10]

In a letter dated September 28, 1878, Father Jules Decorby, O.M.I., described his visit to Father Rappagliosi on the Milk River shortly before Rappagliosi's death:

When I saw the good Father Rappagliosi for the first time I had the impression that he was far from the end of his life. They had just shaved him. His face was a bit gaunt, but cheerful and smiling. I was far from believing that he was so near death. But he was not mistaken about his condition. After we exchanged a few words, he said, Father, since I feel well and in full possession of my senses, I wish to confess. There is no hurry, I answered. No, he said, I feel that my head is unsteady, and since God is granting me a good moment, I want to take advantage of it to put in order the affairs of my soul; and he confessed with all the awareness one may wish for such an important act at the time of death. The following day I was supposed to give him Holy Communion in the form of a viaticum.[11] *But I couldn't do it: The Reverend Father wanted the Holy Mass celebrated in his room: he wanted to be surrounded once more by his dear and faithful parishioners. Unfortunately, as I had feared, the sight of such a crowd come to attend the Mass caused a recurrence of his fever and delirium. He could not receive Holy Communion. The following day I celebrated Mass in a nearby house and right after the Holy Sacrifice I brought him the Holy Viaticum, which he received fully conscious and with feelings of piety and comfort visible in his whole person by those present.*

That day our pious patient seemed to feel better. One might have said that the comfort of that morning had produced a happy change in his state. I believe our Lord doesn't want you with him yet, I said to him smiling: he doesn't yet have enough Indians in Paradise. He replied in the same tone, the fact is I wouldn't mind sending a good group of them there before I myself leave the earth.

Oh, our hopefulness didn't last very long! A few hours later the fever came back higher and more acute than ever. I stayed two more days near our dear patient, giving him all the material care and comfort I could, while receiving in return admirable lessons. . . .

I am terribly sorry that some very particular circumstances forced me to leave the Rev. Father before he breathed his last breath. However urgent those might have been, I would have never agreed to abandon a brother in the situation he was in, if there hadn't been another priest [Genin] there who promised to do everything for his brother on the verge of death.[12]

According to Father Palladino, rumors spread to Rome that Rappagliosi had been poisoned by Genin but an investigation by Col. Edward Moale, then at Fort Benton, failed to substantiate the rumors of foul play. Palladino wrote that the medicine Genin prepared for Rappagliosi "failed to" relieve the patient "as may happen in any sickness, not every remedy proving helpful." The report from Moale's investigation could not be located in the files of the U.S. Adjutant General's Office, the Office of Indian Affairs, or the State Department. The U.S. Army files did contain reports of an investigation of alleged ammunition trading by Genin, but no reports were located relating to Rappagliosi's death.[13]

Biographical Glossary

This glossary includes all individuals named in the letters for whom biographical details could be found, except Rappagliosi family members and local clergy in Rome.

Abraham (-1887). Abraham was chief of the Kootenai band that moved around the Kootenai Valley in a seasonal round that carried it both north and south of the forty-ninth parallel. They finally settled in Bonner's Ferry, Idaho. Abraham was chief from 1869 until he died in 1887. This band was not visited by Rappagliosi.[1]

Agnes (-1884). Originally of the Shoshoni tribe, Agnes was the widow of Victor, the Salish Flathead chief who fought to keep the Bitterroot Valley at the 1855 Hellgate Treaty council. She was Charlo's stepmother. Father Palladino described her as "a woman of excellent parts, clever, industrious, and an example of true Christian piety to all the women of the tribe. Though she was always neater than other Indian women, she looked like an ordinary Indian in her poor garb from the shawl or blanket over her head to her moccasined feet. Nevertheless, her manners manifested the gifted woman that she really was, dignified, sensible, tactful and not only polite but remarkably refined." Victor died in 1870, but Agnes survived until 1884.[2]

Andrew, Peter (-1875). The St. Ignatius "Liber Defunctorum" recorded the burial of twenty-two-year-old Peter Andrew, a Pend d'Oreilles Indian, on February 16, 1875. The son of Peter Andrew and Theresa Maria, he was preceded in death by his mother. He died the day before burial and had received the sacraments of the church.[3]

Arlee, Chief (-1889). Arlee was the chief Rappagliosi attempted to conciliate during his 1875 visit to the Jocko Valley (see letter 20). Arlee objected to the operations of the agency and the St. Ignatius Mission schools. A brave war chief in his younger days, Arlee was Nez

Perce but lived most of his life with the Salish. He was also known as Red Night and Henry. In 1877 Bishop James O'Connor described him as "a noble looking man of about sixty. . . . He wore a white Kossuth hat and a blue blanket, and an eagle's wing hung at his girdle. Obesity had taken all grace from his figure, but I thought I had never seen a finer head or face than his. I could hardly take my eyes off him." In 1883 Arlee complained that one of his sons had been put to work in the harvest field while he was a student at the boys' school in St. Ignatius. Arlee then "indignantly removed him; declaring that he had sent the boy there to learn how to read and write, not to work like a squaw." Arlee died in 1889.[4]

Bandini, Joseph, S.J. (1837-99). An Italian who had a long career as a missionary to the Indians, Bandini was stationed at St. Ignatius in the mid-1870s, where he was responsible, among other things, for visiting the outlying tribes. In the 1880s and 1890s he became well known as a missionary to the Crow Indians. He died in Spokane, Washington.[5]

Baptiste. A Kootenai Indian living with the Piegans, Baptiste acted as in interpreter for Rappagliosi (letters 27-28). In the late 1870s James Willard Schultz recorded travel stories told him by an un-named "Blackfoot-speaking Kootenai, a very aged but still fairly active man" who visited the Blackfoot camp. There is no way to tell if Schultz's Blackfoot-speaking Kootenai was Baptiste. No further information was located about this person.[6]

Beckx, Pierre Jean, S.J. (1795-1887). A Belgian who was father general or head of the Society of Jesus between 1853 and 1883, Beckx placed special emphasis on missions.[7]

Brooks, "Governor" Henry P. (1865-1909). Brooks was an Indian trader at Fort Benton in 1878. Born in Germany, he arrived in Deer Lodge County in 1865 and worked as a miner in various Montana mining camps before becoming a trader. In 1879 he left Fort Benton to begin cattle ranching in the Judith Basin, where he made his fortune.[8]

Charlo, Chief, or Little-Claw-of-a-Grizzly-Bear (1830-1910). Charlo succeeded his father, Victor, in 1870 as chief of the Salish Flatheads.

Charlo continued Victor's efforts to maintain the band's home in the Bitterroot Valley in the face of growing pressures from the government and the surrounding white community. As the buffalo declined, he worked hard to expand the band's farms and stock herds and to avoid conflict with the whites. He had some initial success, but finally, in 1889, drought and poverty forced him to agree to remove to the Jocko Valley on the Flathead Reservation. Father Palladino characterized him as "a man of a quiet yet firm disposition, a true representative of his race and a thorough Indian. . . . His conduct during the Nez Perces outbreak gained him the admiration of all, and proved once more the loyal friendship for the whites on the part of the Flat Heads [sic]. . . . But while friendly toward the whites, he surely is not in love with their ways. . . . Charlot is a sincere and practical Christian." He died in the Jocko in 1910 as the government was forcing the tribe to sell much of the reservation land to white homesteaders.[9]

D'Aste, Jerome, S.J. (1829-1910). An Italian mathematician and priest recruited by Father DeSmet in 1858, D'Aste worked at St. Mary's Mission between 1869 and 1891. When the Flatheads removed to the Flathead Reservation, he transferred to St. Ignatius Mission, where he worked until his death in 1910. D'Aste became close to Chief Charlo.[10]

David (-1891). David was chief of the Kootenai band that lived in the Tobacco Plains area in the Kootenay River Valley, near where Eureka, Montana, was later located, and north into British Columbia. Chief David's daughter, Rowena, married a white Hudson's Bay Company employee and government agent named Michael Phillips in 1866. In 1884 David took part in the frustrating negotiations with the British Columbia government representative for a reserve for the Tobacco Plains band. Chief David died in 1891.[11]

Decorby, Jules, O.M.I. (1841-1916). Decorby was based at the St. Florent Mission at Qu'Appelle, now Labret, Saskatchewan, from 1868 to 1880. He accompanied the Métis on buffalo-hunting expeditions in 1874-75, 1875-76, and 1877-78. Decorby could speak three Indian languages in addition to his native French and three or four other European languages. He was born in France and died in Canada.[12]

DeSmet, Pierre Jean, S.J. (1801-73). DeSmet was a Belgian who became a famous Jesuit missionary and the founder of the Rocky Mountain Mission. In 1838 he founded a mission among the Potawatomi Indians in Iowa. The following year he encountered two Iroquois Indians enroute from the Bitterroot Valley to St. Louis to inquire about missionaries. DeSmet was selected to visit the Flatheads in 1840. In 1841 he returned and established St. Mary's Mission in the Bitterroot Valley. He founded other mission stations in the Rocky Mountains and raised money to support the missionaries. These activities made him well known among the Indian people of the Northwest and the larger American public.[13]

Diomedi, Alexander, S.J. (1843-1932). An Italian, Diomedi taught and studied at Tivoli and the Roman College in the 1860s. In 1874 he came to the United States and studied printing, and in 1875 he arrived at St. Ignatius to operate the printing press and instruct some of the Indian students in printing. In 1877 he was transferred to work with the Coeur d'Alene Indians. In later years he did pastoral and educational work in various churches in the Pacific Northwest, California, and even Brazil. He died in Washington State in 1932.[14]

Genin, Jean Baptiste Marie, O.M.I. (1837-1900). See the biographical information about Genin in appendix B.

Giorda, Joseph, S.J., (1823-82). An Italian, Giorda was superior general of the Rocky Mountain Mission between 1862 and 1866 and 1869 and 1877. During this period he greatly expanded the Indian missions in the northern Rockies, which had previously been reduced in order to expand the missions in California. His headquarters was at St. Ignatius.[15]

Good Woman or Arsapaki (-1878). Known as Generous Woman in the agency records, this Piegan chief was the leader of the Grease Melters Band. A good warrior, Good Woman had four wives. He was elected second chief during the winter of 1875. According to the agency records, White Calf was elected head chief after the death of Little Plume in August 1877, but elderly Blackfeet in the 1940s understood that Good Woman succeeded Little Plume as head chief of the Piegans. Good Woman died on October 21, 1878.[16]

Grassi, Urban, S.J. (1830–90). Grassi taught at Jesuit colleges in California before arriving at St. Ignatius Mission in 1861. He was stationed at St. Ignatius between 1861 and 1869 and at several missions in Washington Territory between 1869 and 1879. During the 1870s he also made some trips to the Indian tribes in northern Montana.[17]

Guidi, Joseph, S.J. (1842–1908). Father Guidi was the author of the obituary and biography of Rappagliosi that appeared in Woodstock Letters (reprinted in appendix A). He was born in Italy and entered the Society of Jesus in 1859. References in the letters indicate that Guidi knew Rappagliosi and Rappagliosi's family in Italy before he came to the United States.

In the summer of 1872 Guidi arrived at St. Mary's Mission after a two-month trip by riverboat between St. Louis and Fort Benton. In 1873 Guidi was at St. Ignatius studying the English and Salish languages. By 1874, when Rappagliosi arrived in Montana Territory, Guidi had been assigned as a minister to St. Francis Regis Mission near Fort Colville in Washington Territory, where he remained through 1876. In 1877 he joined Rappagliosi at St. Peter's Mission and studied the Blackfeet language until September, when poor health forced him to leave. During most of 1877, when Rappagliosi was visiting various Indian and white groups in northern Montana, Guidi resided at Rappagliosi's home base at St. Peter's Mission.

Guidi worked in Helena and at St. Ignatius and St. Joseph's Mission among the Nez Perce Indians between 1878 and 1899. Ironically, Guidi returned to St. Mary's after the removal of Charlo's band of Salish Flatheads, when the mission had become a parish church for the local white settlers. He was transferred to Brazil in 1899. In 1902 he was ministering to the English-speaking Catholics in Sao Paulo, Brazil. He died in that city in 1908. Father Guidi's command of Salish must have been considerable, as he was listed as one of the contributing authors of the Salish or Kalispel Indian dictionary printed at St. Ignatius during the late 1870s.[18]

Ignatius, or Eneas Paul Big Knife (1828-1900). Ignatius was chief of the Kootenai band that lived in various locations in western Montana over the years. In the 1870s the band lived primarily in the Upper Flathead Valley and on Flathead Lake. In the late nineteenth century it moved to Elmo, which was on Flathead Lake and within the Flathead Reservation. Ignatius was devoted to his people and highly respected by the church and agency. He helped the Kootenais develop subsistence agriculture to replace the buffalo hunt. His band was not visited by Father Rappagliosi during his trip.[19]

Ignatius, Paul. Rappagliosi called this man the chief of the Signeses (letter 11). He was possibly a chief of the Lake Indians from the Arrow Lakes and Kettle River area of British Columbia and Washington. No information was located about this chief.

Imoda, John Baptist Camillus, S.J. (1829-86). An Italian, Imoda worked at St. Peter's Mission and St. Ignatius Mission and in Helena. Except for some short assignments to St. Ignatius, Imoda was at St. Peter's most of the time between 1859 and 1880. He was superior or head of the St. Peter's Mission during the late 1870s, when Rappagliosi was stationed there.[20]

Joseph. Joseph was chief of the Cranbrook, British Columbia, area Kootenai band. According to David McLaughlin, a Hudson's Bay Company trader among the Kootenai, Joseph was born among the Lower Kootenai but rose to become chief of the Upper Kootenai at Cranbrook through his abilities as a warrior. In 1861 Charles Wilson observed a Kootenai chief named Joseph who had a small farm with a band of seventy head of horses and thirty head of cattle. In 1870 R. L. T. Galbraith reported that Michel was the head chief and Joseph the second chief. By 1874, when Rappagliosi visited the band, Joseph was head chief and Moses the second chief. Joseph's son, Isadore, was chief of the band in the mid-1880s during the friction over land rights and white settlers' charges of murder against a Kootenai Indian. The area around Cranbrook was known as Joseph's Prairie.[21]

Koitó, Moses (-1875). Koitó was the Pend d'Oreilles Indian who died from the effects of freezing (letter 18). The "Liber Defunctorum" for St. Ignatius Mission recorded the burial of Moses Koitó on January 15, 1875. He was about seventy-five years old and had received the sacraments just before his death.[22]

Lattanzi, Sanctus, S.J. (1837-1903). An Italian, Lattanzi entered the Jesuit order in 1858. In 1879 and 1880 he was assigned to St. Peter's Mission as a student of the Blackfeet language. He returned to Rome in June 1880 because of his health. He died in Rome.[23]

Liguori, Alphonsus, St. (1696-1787). An Italian Roman Catholic theologian who founded the Redemptorist order, Liguori was canonized in 1839.

Little Feather (-1877). Little Feather, known as Little Plume, was chief of the Worm Band of the Piegans and in 1875 was elected chief of the entire Piegan tribe. Also known as White Buffalo Chief, Little Plume was remembered as "a warrior" and "was very well liked." He was "a very large, fat man" with "a good presence and winning ways." Little Plume fought against forced reductions in the reservation and opposed the white whiskey traders. He courteously listened to the Jesuit priests, but he also was a friend of Rev. William Van Orsdel, the Methodist minister known as "Brother Van." He died August 22, 1877, when he was only a little over forty years old.[24]

Melchers, Brother Joseph, S.J. (1845-80). A German, Melchers entered the order in 1870. In March 1874, Rappagliosi said Melcher was at St. Mary's, but Melcher was listed as working in Helena in 1874. In 1875 he was transferred to the Sacred Heart Mission among the Coeur d'Alene Indians, where he worked as a carpenter. He died in 1880 at Santa Clara, California.[25]

Michelle (1805-97). Michelle was head chief of the Upper Pend d'Oreilles Indians whose home village was at St. Ignatius Mission. During the middle 1870s he was physically unable to accompany the tribe on their seasonal buffalo hunts on the Plains and lost much of his influence to Andre, the second chief. During the 1870s Michelle lived near the agency in the Jocko Valley, while most of his tribe remained near St. Ignatius Mission to the north. Later he moved to a ranch on Mud Creek near Ronan. He was reported to be a severe disciplinarian who encouraged the Pend d' Oreilles to establish farms.[26]

Moses. Moses succeeded Joseph as second chief of the Cranbrook band of Kootenai Indians in the early 1870s. Shortly before Rappagliosi's visit to Joseph's camp during the summer of 1874, a large group of Upper Kootenai buffalo hunters fought the white traders and the Blackfeet at Fort Macleod. Fighting broke out as the Kootenai attempted to put out a grass fire near the fort, which they were inaccurately accused of starting. Moses rode among the Kootenai and counseled them to retreat for the sake of their families, who depended on them. The Kootenai withdrew to their homes west of the mountains.[27]

Negro, Brother John, S.J. (1841–1912). An Italian, Negro was transferred from St. Ignatius Mission in 1876 to work on the farm at St. Peter's, where he was stationed until 1889. He spent the last years of his life at St. Joseph's Mission among the Nez Perce Indians.[28]

O'Flinn, Peter, S.J. (1822–1907). O'Flinn, an Irishman, entered the Jesuit order in 1869 and died in Melbourne, Australia.[29]

Pius IX (1792–1878). Pius was pope from 1846 to 1878. A conservative pope, he struggled to maintain control of the Papal States and prevent Italian unification. Between 1848 and 1850 he lived in exile in Gaeta in the Kingdom of Naples. Between 1850 and 1870 French military forces supported the pope's restored government. In 1870 the pope finally lost control of Rome and spent the rest of his rule as a voluntary prisoner in the Vatican. Pius was a strong supporter of missions and a more centralized church government.

Ragazzini, Pietro, S.J. (1827–77). An Italian, Ragazzini was father provincial or head of the Roman Province between 1872 and 1876. Ragazzini entered the order in 1851 and served as rector for the Roman College or Gregorian University before and after his tenure as provincial.[30]

Scollen, Constantine, O.M.I. (1841-1902). Scollen was born in Ireland and served for many years as a missionary in Alberta. Between 1873 and 1882 he was based at a mission to the Blackfeet where Calgary is now located. Between 1873 and 1881 he also ministered at Fort Macleod. He died in 1902 in Dayton, Ohio.[31]

Susanna (-1874). Susanna was the Salish Indian who died in the Bitterroot. According to the "Liber Mortuorum" for St. Mary's, Susanna died on April 24, 1874, shortly after confessing. She was the wife of Dominic the lame.[32]

Three Chiefs. Three Chiefs was a Piegan Indian and the son of Good Woman. The first two censuses of the Montana Blackfeet, both done in 1890, list three sons of Arsapaki or Good Woman: Weasel Fat, thirty-five years old; Earring, thirty-five years old; and Three Chiefs, twenty-seven years old. Three Chiefs would have been thirteen in 1876. In 1890 he was unmarried and living with his older brother, Weasel Fat or Obasis, and his sister-in-law, Good Shield. Three Chiefs did not appear in the later censuses.[33]

Weekly, Alexander. Weekly was a Métis. The 1880 census lists Alex Wilky and family in the Judith Basin of Montana Territory, where the family had moved in 1879. Alex Wilky was listed as a forty-nine-year-old Indian farmer; his wife, Louisa, was a fifty-year-old housekeeper; and their four daughters were Julia (twenty-two years), Louse (fifteen years), Varonceta (eleven years), and Mary (seven years). Joseph Kinsey Howard reports that Alexander Wilkie was a leader of the Judith Basin Métis community: "Daily prayers were customary in the homes and the children went to Alexander Wilkie, builder of the big house, for regular religious instruction. Wilkie, member of a family whose men had been leaders among the *Bois-Brules* from earliest times of the race was a musician, too – a singer and violinist. From the youngsters of the colony he built a choir and trained it in liturgical music he had learned at St. Boniface and Pembina."[34]

Williams, Captain Constant, U.S.A. (1843-1922). Williams was a witness to Rappagliosi's death. He was stationed at Fort Benton, and on February 6, 1878, he reported that he was going to the Métis settlement the next day to tell them that they did not have a right to settle on the reservation and were subject to removal. Williams had seen action at the Battle of the Big Hole, where he was wounded twice. He retired as a brigadier general in 1907.[35]

Xavier, St. Francis, S.J. (1506–52). Xavier was a famous Jesuit missionary to India and Japan. One of the seven original companions of Ignatius in 1534, he established a very successful mission in southern India, primarily among the lower castes. From India he went on to Malaya and Japan. He founded the Japanese Christian church in 1549, and at the time of his death he was attempting to gain entry to China. Xavier is the patron saint of the missions and consequently received special devotion from Father Rappagliosi.

Abbreviations

ARCIA   *Annual Report of the Commissioner of Indian Affairs.* Washington DC.

ARSI   *Annual Report of the Secretary of the Interior.* Washington DC.

Bischoff   William N. Bischoff, S.J. *The Jesuits in Old Oregon.* Caldwell ID: Caxton, 1945.

Brown   Ellsworth Howard Brown. "The History of the Flathead Indians in the Nineteenth Century." Ph.D. diss., Michigan State University, 1975.

Carrière   Gaston Carrière. *Dictionnaire biographique des Oblats de Marie-Immaculée au Canada.* Ottawa ON: Éditions de l'Université d'Ottawa, 1976-89.

Catalogus   *Catalogus Dispersae Provinciae Taurinensis Societatis Iesu.* Monoeci: Ex typographia Scholastica. In 1878 the title changed to *Catalogus Sociorum et Officiorum Provinciae Taurinensis Societatis Iesu.*

CIA   Commissioner of Indian Affairs

Grassi   Urban Grassi, S.J. "Kootenais." *Annals of the Propagation of the Faith* (Dublin, Ireland) 36, no. 1 (Jan. 1873): 305-11.

HNAI   *Handbook of North American Indians.* Washington DC, 1978- .

Memorie   Filippo Rappagliosi, S.J. *Memorie del P. Filippo Rappagliosi, D.C.D.G., missionario apostolico nelle Montagne Rocciose.* Rome: Bernardo Morini, 1879.

Mendizábal   P. Rufo Mendizábal, S.J. *Catalogus defunctorum in renata Societate Iesu ab a. 1814 ad a. 1970.* Rome: apud Curiam P. Gen., 1972.

Montana   *Montana: The Magazine of Western History*

NAmf   National Archives Microfilm Publication

NAmf234   U.S. Office of Indian Affairs. *Letters Received by Office of Indian Affairs, 1874-81.* National Archives Microfilm Publication M234.

NAmf666   U.S. Office of the Adjutant General. *Letters Received by the*

Office of the Adjutant General, Main Series, 1871–1880. National Archives Microfilm Publication M666.

NYFJ   *New York Freeman's Journal and Catholic Register*

O'Connor   Rev. James O'Connor. "The Flathead Indians." *Records of the American Catholic Historical Society of Philadelphia* 3 (1889–91): 85–110.

OPA   Oregon Province Archives of the Society of Jesus, Foley Library, Gonzaga University, Spokane, Wash.

Palladino   L. B. Palladino, S.J. *Indian and White in the Northwest: A History of Catholicity in Montana, 1831–1891,* 2nd ed. Lancaster PA: Wickersham Publishing, 1922.

PNTMC   Robert C. Carriker and Eleanor R. Carriker, eds. *Microfilm Edition of the Pacific Northwest Tribes Missions Collection of the Oregon Province Archives of the Society of Jesus.* Wilmington DE: Scholarly Resources,, 1987.

Ronan   Mary Ronan. *Frontier Woman: The Story of Mary Ronan as Told to Margaret Ronan.* Ed. H. G. Merriam. Missoula: University of Montana Publications in History, 1973.

Slaughter   Linda W. Slaughter. "Leaves from Northwestern History." In *Collections of the State Historical Society of North Dakota,* 1:200–292. Bismark ND, 1906.

Smyth   Fred J. Smyth. *Tales of the Kootenays,* 2nd ed. Cranbrook BC: The Courier, 1942.

Spry   Irene M. Spry, ed. *The Papers of the Palliser Expedition, 1857–1860.* Toronto ON: Champlain Society, 1968.

Teit   James A. Teit. "The Salishan Tribes of the Western Plateaus." In *Annual Report of the Bureau of American Ethnology, 1927–28,* 295–396. Washington DC, 1930.

WM   Missoula MT *Weekly Missoulian*

Notes

INTRODUCTION

1. On the Salish Flatheads in the 1870s, see: Robert Bigart, "The Salish Flathead Indians during the Period of Adjustment, 1850-1891," *Idaho Yesterdays* 17, no. 3 (fall 1973): 18-28; Brown; James William Carroll, "Flatheads and Whites: A Study of Conflict" (Ph.D. diss., University of California, Berkeley, 1959); J. Verne Dusenberry, "Samples of Pend d'Oreille Oral Literature and Salish Narratives," in *Lifeways of Intermontane and Plains Montana Indians*, ed. Leslie B. Davis (Bozeman MT: Museum of the Rockies, Montana State University, 1979), 109-20; John Fahey, *The Flathead Indians* (Norman: University of Oklahoma Press, 1974), 149-226; Anthony McGinnis, *Counting Coup and Cutting Horses: Intertribal Warfare on the Northern Plains, 1738-1889* (Evergreen CO: Cordillera, 1990), 129-71.

2. M. C. Page to Alphonso Taft, Dec. 28, 1876, NAmf234, reel 508, frames 391-95.

3. *Deer Lodge MT Weekly Independent*, Aug. 24, 1872, p. 2, col. 7.

4. See Shirley Jay Coon, "The Economic Development of Missoula, Montana" (Ph.D. diss., University of Chicago, 1926), 56-125.

5. *wm*, Aug. 20, 1874, p. 2, col. 2-3. See also *wm*, May 28, 1874, p. 2, col. 2, and various stories in 1877 at the start of the Nez Perce crisis in the Bitterroot Valley, such as *wm*, June 29, 1877, p. 2, col. l.

6. C. S. Jones to Jasper A. Viall, Sept. 1, 1871, *arsi*, 1871, 841.

7. [Chief Charlo], "Indian Taxation" *wm*, Apr. 26, 1876, p. 3, col. 3-4.

8. On St. Mary's Mission, see: Cornelius M. Buckley, S.J., *Nicolas Point, S.J.: His Life & Northwest Indian Chronicles* (Chicago: Loyola University Press, 1989); Robert C. Carriker, *Father Peter John De Smet: Jesuit in the West* (Norman: University of Oklahoma Press, 1995), 31-62; Lucylle H. Evans, *St. Mary's in the Rocky Mountains: A History of the Cradle of Montana's Culture*, rev. ed. (Stevensville MT: Montana Creative Consultants, 1976); J. Michael Moyer, S.J., "Missionary-Indian Alienation at Saint Mary's Mission, 1841 to 1850," (Gonzaga University, Spokane WA, 1961, photocopied student paper); Palladino, 41-90; Claude E. Schaeffer, "The First

Jesuit Mission to the Flathead, 1840–1850: A Study in Culture Conflicts," *Pacific Northwest Quarterly* 28, no. 3 (July 1937): 227–50.

9. On the Flathead Indian Reservation in the 1870s, see: Brown, 198–353; Fahey, *Flathead Indians*, 149–226; Ronald Lloyd Trosper, "The Economic Impact of the Allotment Policy on the Flathead Indian Reservation" (Ph.D. diss., Harvard University, 1974).

10. Brown, 260–71; Chas S. Medary to CIA, Sept. 13, 1875, *arcia*, 1875, 304–7.

11. James A. Garfield, "Report of Hon. James A. Garfield, Commissioner for the Removal of the Flathead Tribe of Indians from the Bitter Root Valley in Montana Territory . . ." *arcia*, 1872, 114.

12. Report from Inspector J. W. Daniels to CIA, Nov. 13, 1873, Inspection Reports File, Bureau of Indian Affairs Papers, RG 75, National Archives, Washington DC.

13. Alley Quill-quill-squa to U. S. Grant, Nov. 1, 1874, NAmf234, reel 500, frames 190–95.

14. On St. Ignatius Mission, see: *100 Years in the Flathead Valley: The St. Ignatius Centennial* (St. Ignatius MT: n.p., 1954); Brown, 333–53; William L. Davis, S.J., *A History of St. Ignatius Mission* (Spokane WA: C. W. Hill, 1954); Gilbert J. Garraghan, S.J., *The Jesuits of the Middle United States* (New York: America Press, 1938), 2:256–441; Palladino, 91–184.

15. Chas. S. Medary to CIA, Sept. 13, 1875, *arcia*, 1875, 304–7.

16. Palladino, 98; O'Connor, 94.

17. O'Connor, 103.

18. On Canadian Kootenai Indians in the 1870s, see: Robin Fisher, *Contact and Conflict: Indian-European Relations in British Columbia, 1774–1890*, 2nd ed. (Vancouver BC: UBC Press, 1992); Smyth, 70–71; Harry Holbert Turney-High, *Ethnography of the Kutenai*, Memoir of the American Anthropological Association No. 56 (Mensasha WI, 1941), 9–55.

19. Spry, 462; George Gibbs, ""Physical Geography of the North-Western Boundary of the United States," *Journal of the American Geographical Society of New York* 3 (1872): 381–82.

20. Isaac I. Stevens, "Report of Explorations for a Route for the Pacific Railroad from St. Paul to Puget Sound," in *Reports of Explorations and Surveys for a Railroad Route from the Mississippi River to the Pacific Ocean*, 33rd Cong., 2nd sess., 1855, H. Ex. Doc. 91, serial 791, 1:418, 443. On Piegan ethnography and Piegan affairs in the 1870s, see: John C. Ewers, *The Horse in Blackfoot Indian Culture, with Comparative Materials from Other*

Western Tribes, Bureau of American Ethnology Bulletin 159 (Washington DC, 1955); John C. Ewers, *The Blackfeet: Raiders of the Northwestern Plains* (Norman: University of Oklahoma Press, 1958), 226–96; John C. Ewers, "Ethnological Report on the Blackfeet and Gros Ventres Tribes of Indians," in *Blackfeet Indians* (New York: Garland, 1974), 23–202; Thomas R. Wessel, "Historical Report on the Blackfeet Reservation in Northern Montana" (U.S. Indian Claims Commission, Washington DC, 1975), docket 279-D, photocopied report.

21. On St. Peter's Mission, see: Palladino, 185–229; Wilfred P. Schoenberg, S.J., "Historic St. Peter's Mission: Landmark of the Jesuits and the Ursulines among the Blackfeet," *Montana* 11, no. 1 (winter 1961): 68–85.

22. On the Métis in the 1870s, see: Verne Dusenberry, "Waiting for a Day that Never Comes," *Montana* 8, no. 2 (Apr. 1958): 26–39; Marcel Giraud, *The Metis in the Canadian West* (Lincoln: University of Nebraska Press, 1986), 2:211–524; Julia D. Harrison, *Metis: People between Two Worlds* (Vancouver BC: Glenbow-Alberta Institute and Douglas & McIntyre, 1985); Joseph Kinsey Howard, *Strange Empire: A Narrative of the Northwest* (New York: William Morrow, 1952); Slaughter; Bill Thackeray, ed., *The Metis Centennial Celebration Publication, 1879–1979* (Lewistown MT: Metis Centennial Celebration Committee, 1979); NAmf666, reel 362, file 4976 AGO 1877, frames 2–302.

23. Guidi's quote is from *Memorie,* 20.

24. Most of the biographical information for this sketch came from *Memorie.* Additional sources are noted in the following notes.

25. [Joseph Guidi, S.J.], "Obituary: Father Philip Rappagliosi," *Woodstock Letters* 8, no. 2 (1879): 97; "Burial of a Priest," *Helena MT Daily Herald,* Feb. 18, 1878, p. 3, col. 3; Bischoff, 230; Schoenberg, "Historic St. Peter's Mission," 81.

26. Vittorio Spreti, ed., *Enciclopedia Storico-nobiliare Italiana,* 6 vols. (Milan: Ed. Enciclopedia Storico-nobiliare Italiana, 1928–32).

1. CALLING TO THE SOCIETY OF JESUS

1. A novena is the recitation of prayers and practicing of devotions during a nine-day period, usually to mark a saint's feast day or for specific requests. Novenas were important in lay piety.

The matter to which Rappagliosi refers is his intention to join the Society of Jesus.

2. THE CALL TO BE A MISSIONARY

1. Tronchiennes is the French name for Drongen, a Belgian village near Ghent.
2. P.C. stands for "Pax Christi," Latin for "Peace of Christ [to you]." Ignatius, the founder of the Society of Jesus, used this in his letters, and it is generally used by Jesuits.
3. July 31 is St. Ignatius's feast day and thus a great celebration. It marks the day Ignatius died. Rappagliosi's interest in saints' days and his use of spiritual signs or omens to confirm his missionary work were expressions of popular Catholic culture in nineteenth-century Europe.
   The father provincial was Pietro Ragazzini, S.J., and the reverend father general was Pierre Jean Beckx, S.J. For biographical information, see appendix C.
4. The exercises that Rappagliosi mentions are the Spiritual Exercises of St. Ignatius, used by all Jesuits.
5. "Propaganda" is the Sacred Congregation for the Propagation of the Faith, the department of the Roman Curia charged with administration of the church's missionary activities. *New Catholic Encyclopedia*, 1967 ed., s.v. "Propagation of the Faith, Congregation for the."

3. ON THE SAME TOPIC

1. The feast of the Exaltation of the Holy Cross is celebrated on September 14.
2. After he wrote these letters he went to Rome to give his last farewell to his relatives. From there he left in October to start his journey to the mission to which he had been assigned. – 1879 editor.

4. TRAVELS IN ENGLAND

1. Aix la Chappelle is the French name for Aachen, Germany.
2. Here Rappagliosi wrote, literally, "I didn't pay a toll to the sea." – Trans.
3. Queenstown was the southern Irish port now called Cobh.
4. Founded in 1425 by bull of Pope Martin V, Louvain was closed during the Napoleonic Wars but reopened in 1834. In 1970 it was separated into two universities: Universite Catholique de Louvain, with instruction in French, and Katholieke Universiteit Leuven, with instruction in Dutch

and English. *International Handbook of Universities and Other Institutions of Higher Education*, 11th ed. (New York: Stockton, 1989), 37–38.

5. Built in Ireland, the *Celtic* was owned by the White Star Line and had its maiden voyage in 1872. It was powered by both steam and sail, with four masts and one funnel. Tonnage was 3,888, and dimensions were 437 feet by 40 feet. It was scrapped in 1898. Eugene W. Smith, *Passenger Ships of the World, Past and Present* (Boston MA: George H. Dean, 1963), 52.

6. Rappagliosi signed most of these letters "Miss. Apost." There was a formal honorary office called missionary apostolic that the pope bestowed on a few select missionaries, but none of the sources suggest Rappagliosi had this formal title. Presumably the closing meant he was a missionary who, like the first apostles, went out to a far land to preach the gospel of Christ.

5. DEPARTURE FOR AMERICA

1. Rappagliosi later gave the name of the German who roomed with them as Roettger. This person did not appear in the catalog of Jesuit deaths from 1814 to 1970 and also was not listed as a priest in either the United States or Canada in *Sadliers' Catholic Directory Almanac . . . for 1883* (New York: D. & J. Sadlier & Co., 1883).

6. TRANSATLANTIC CROSSING AND ARRIVAL IN NEW YORK

1. The College of St. Francis Xavier is now Fordham University in the Bronx, New York. First established in 1841, it was transferred to the Society of Jesus in 1846 and became an independent institution in 1969. It was renamed Fordham University in 1907. *American Universities and Colleges*, 13th ed. (New York: Walter deGruyter, 1987), 1138–40.

2. Sandy Hook Bay is formed by a peninsula in eastern New Jersey at the south entrance of New York Harbor. The harbor is about twenty miles south of Manhattan.

3. *La Chartreuse de Parma* is an herbal liqueur made by the Carthesian monks near Grenoble, France. Formulated from 130 herbs, it has been promoted as a heal-all tonic since the 16th century.

Acqua della Scala is a lavender water in the Discalced Carmelites' herbal line made in Italy. It is advertised as a remedy for numerous ailments. Antonino Lo Nardo, e-mail to Bigart, Aug. 19, 2004.

7. JOURNEY FROM NEW YORK TO ST. LOUIS

1. St. Francis Regis Mission, to which Father Guidi was assigned, occupied various locations between Kettle Falls and Colville in northeastern Washington after 1869. From this station the priests visited tribes from north-central Washington to northern Idaho, including the Kootenai Indians. Bischoff, 156–62.
2. The college in Baltimore is now known as Loyola College. It was established in 1852 and has been operated by the Society of Jesus since then. *American Universities and Colleges*, 753–55.
3. A seminary of the Society of Jesus was established in 1869 at Woodstock, Maryland, a small town about fourteen miles west of downtown Baltimore. The *Woodstock Letters*, a major source for American Jesuit history, was published there between 1872 and 1969. The seminary was closed about 1970. Leon E. Seltzer, ed., *Columbia Lippincott Gazetteer of the World* (New York: Columbia University Press, 1952), 2105; *Yearbook of Higher Education 1970* (Los Angeles CA: Academic Media, 1970), 157.

8. JOURNEY TO AND ARRIVAL AT THE ROCKY MOUNTAINS

1. Corinne, Utah Territory, north of the Great Salt Lake, was the station on the Union Pacific Railroad closest to Montana Territory. In 1873 travelers would go by rail to Corinne and then by stagecoach to Montana.
2. The diligences were public stagecoaches formerly much used in France and other European countries.
3. Helena was born as a gold-mining camp in Last Chance Gulch in 1864. By 1870 it was the largest city in Montana Territory, with over thirty-one hundred residents. By 1873 when Rappagliosi arrived, it had a Roman Catholic church with two priests, a school, and a hospital operated by the Sisters of Charity of Leavenworth, Kansas. On January 9, 1874,

shortly after Rappagliosi left for St. Mary's Mission, much of Helena was destroyed in a large fire. In 1875 the rebuilt city became the capital of Montana Territory. In 1878 Rappagliosi was buried in the Church of the Sacred Hearts in Helena. Vivian Paladin and Jean Baucus, *Helena: An Illustrated History* (Norfolk VA: Donning, 1983), 26–35; Palladino, 315–37; "Burial of a Priest," *Helena Daily Herald*, Feb. 18, 1878, p. 3, col. 3.

4. *Te Deum* refers to a religious service in which an old Christian hymn beginning "Te Deum laudamus" [We praise thee, O God] is a main feature.

9. FIRST NEWS FROM THE MISSIONS

1. Father Palladino's history of the Catholic church in Montana records an incident from Rappagliosi's 1873–74 respite in Helena that is not mentioned in the letters. As Rappagliosi was leaving Helena for St. Mary's in January 1874, he stopped by St. John's Hospital to say goodbye to Palladino, who had been watching to keep a patient from leaving the hospital. During the night the patient borrowed Palladino's shoes and slipped out the window while Palladino slept. Rappagliosi entered the room in the morning and was able to share the amusement about Palladino's lost patient. Palladino, 214–17.

2. The woman Rappagliosi mentions here is Agnes, the widow of Victor, the Salish Flathead chief who fought to keep the Bitterroot Valley at the 1855 Hellgate Treaty council.

3. The cone-shaped hut that Rappagliosi described was a buffalo-skin tepee, which was commonly used by tribes in the Great Plains area. A tepee was light and portable and could be erected by one person in about fifteen minutes. Harry Holbert Turney-High, *The Flathead Indians of Montana*, American Anthropological Association Memoir No. 48 (Menasha WI, 1937), 99–102.

4. Carlo was more commonly known as Chief Charlo. The coincidence is that Rappagliosi's parents were named Agnese and Carlo.

10. CUSTOMS OF THE INDIANS

1. According to the baptismal book for St. Mary's, Mary Ann, born January 1874 to Samuel and Mary, was baptized on February 8, 1874, by Father

Rappagliosi in Missoula. No tribal affiliation was given, and the earliest (1886) census for the Flathead Reservation and Bitterroot Flatheads contained no reference to this family. "St. Mary's Mission, Montana: 'Index to Baptisms at St. Mary's Mission Bitter Root Valley, 1866–1894,'" *pntmc*, reel 1, frame 112.

11. FIRST GOOD DEEDS

1. March 19 is St. Joseph's feast day.
2. The Crow Indians lived on a part of the Great Plains that is now southeastern Montana. They spoke a Siouan language and traded, fought, and even allied with the Salish at different times during the late nineteenth century. Robert H. Lowie, *The Crow Indians* (New York: Holt, Rinehart and Winston, 1935).
3. The Nez Perce Indians were close allies and neighbors of the Salish. They spoke a Sahaptian language that was very different from Salish but joined the Salish in Plains buffalo hunts. Deward Walker Jr., "Nez Perce," *hnai*, 12:420–38; Turney-High, *Flathead Indians*, 136–38; Teit, 322–25.

   The Snake or Shoshone Indians lived in eastern Idaho, south of the Bitterroot Valley. They spoke a different language but joined the Salish in buffalo hunts on the Plains, and intermarriage between the tribes was common. Robert F. Murphy and Yolanda Murphy, "Northern Shoshone and Bannack," *hnai*, 11:262–83.

12. PIOUSNESS OF THE CATHOLIC INDIANS AT EASTER

1. The Italian quoted here is ungrammatical but understandable. – Trans.
2. The Gloria is the Latin hymn in praise of God that begins with *gloria* and is sung in the Mass. The Credo is the Apostles' Creed or the Nicene Creed, both of which begin with *credo*.
3. *Regina coeli* is Latin for "Queen of Heaven," the opening words of a hymn or chant said during the Easter season. Albert J. Nevins, M.M., *The Maryknoll Catholic Dictionary* (New York: Grosset & Dunlap, 1965), 485.

4. The editor could not identify the family with the sick girl and blind old woman, nor was any further information located about Michael.

13. WAY OF LIFE AMONG THE INDIANS AND GOOD DEEDS

1. The "Nuns of Missoula" were the Sisters of Charity of Providence, headquartered in Montreal. Starting in 1873 the sisters operated a school and hospital in Missoula. Palladino, 362-74.

2. The Trevi is a fountain in Rome commissioned by Pope Clement XII in 1735 and designed by Niccolo Salvi. William P. P. Longfellow, ed., *A Cyclopaedia of Works of Architecture in Italy, Greece, and the Levant* (New York: Charles Scribner's Sons, 1895), 351-52.

3. It was the custom in the Tridentine Mass to cleanse the chalice as well as the four fingers that would have touched the host with wine and then wine and water. Thus the dispensation to use water alone for the second cleansing conserved on the use of wine.

4. Pi lu' ye kin, a Nez Perce who lived in the Bitterroot Valley in the 1870s, described the economy of the Nez Perces whom Rappagliosi met. These Nez Perces lived in the Bitterroot, hunted and traded on the Plains, and traded dried buffalo meat for roots harvested by other Nez Perces in Idaho. Anthony E. Thomas, *Pi lu' ye kin: The Life History of a Nez Perce Indian* (Washington DC: American Anthropological Association, 1970).

5. Rappagliosi describes the death of a woman named Susanna. Later in this same letter he describes her funeral feast.

6. Absolution is the forgiveness or remission of sin granted by a priest after penance.

7. The baptismal records for St. Mary's indicate that on May 1, 1874, a son was born to Peter Snaze and Rosalie, and on the same day he was baptized Philip by Father Rappagliosi at St. Mary's. No record of the family was found in the 1886 census of the Flathead Reservation or the Bitterroot Flathead band. "St. Mary's Mission Montana: 'Index to Baptisms at St. Mary's Mission Bitter Root Valley, 1866-1894,'" pntmc, reel 1, frame 120.

8. In 1871 a correspondent for the *Missoula Pioneer* described two very similar funeral feasts in the Bitterroot Valley. The article described a general feast to which everyone was invited and where speeches of condolence

were given and the decedent's property was distributed. In the 1871 case the deaths had taken place on the plains, but the feasts were held after the tribe returned to the Bitterroot Valley. *Missoula MT Pioneer,* Aug. 10, 1871, p. 3, col. 2.

9. The Coeur d'Alene Indians lived in the area of northern Idaho surrounding Coeur d'Alene Lake. They regularly hunted and traded with the Bitterroot Salish, and intermarriage with the Salish was common. Teit, 37–197.

Although Rappagliosi states that the Flatheads and Coeur d'Alenes speak the same language, in fact, the Coeur d'Alene and Kalispel languages are related members of the Salish language family but are not mutually intelligible. M. Dale Kinkade, et al., "Languages," *hnai,* 12:48–77.

14. ATTITUDES OF THE INDIANS

1. In the nineteenth century the feast of St. Philip, the apostle, was celebrated on May 1.

16. DRESS, LIVING ARRANGEMENTS, AND FOODS

1. Rappagliosi's wording is not entirely clear: "c'è qualche cosa di bianco," literally "when there is something white." – Trans.
2. In describing his ripped pants, Rappagliosi uses an expression that has no literal translation in English. – Trans.

17. MISSION TO THE CANADIAN KOOTENAI TRIBE

This letter was published in English in the *Annals of the Propagation of the Faith* (Dublin, Ireland) 40, no. 1 (Jan. 1877): 231–36. The spelling has been modernized.

1. Kalispels was another name for the Pend d'Oreilles Indians at St. Ignatius Mission.
2. What Rappagliosi referred to as the Hanging-Ears River is now known as the Flathead River.
3. A league is a measure of distance that varied in different times and countries but usually measured about three miles.

4. The church building at Tobacco Plains was probably the one built by the Kootenais in spring 1857. James M. Alden saw it in 1860 and described the church as "entirely empty, except some religious engravings; there was a picture of Pius IX and of saints. I recognized it as a church by its form, and it was so spoken of. It was not chinked so as to be suitable for a store or dwelling-house, and the light was received within through the chinks. It was constructed of logs. You could see daylight through the roof, which was apparently of bark covered with mud. It was of one story. It was a long narrow building, at least thirty feet long, but the length much greater than the breadth." A letter from Father Urban Grassi, S.J., however, seemed to suggest that Grassi chose the site for a chapel at Tobacco Plains in 1871. He reported in 1872 that the Tobacco Plains Kootenai had "built a nice little chapel, where, within four walls formed of trunks of trees laid one upon another, we were able more comfortably to go through our religious exercises." Spry, 572; British and American Joint Commission for the Final Settlement of the Claims of the Hudson's Bay and Puget's Sound Agricultural Companies [papers] (Washington DC and Montreal QC: U.S. Government Printing Office and J. Lovel, 1865–69), 9:552–53; Grassi, 310.

5. Thomas Blakiston visited the Tobacco Plains Kootenai band in 1858 and observed: "They are nearly all baptized Roman Catholics, and are most particular in their attendance at morning and evening prayers, to which they are summoned by a small handbell. They always pray before eating. On the Sunday I spent with them their service, in which is a good deal of singing, lasted considerable time. One of their number preached, and seemed to be well attended to." Spry, 575.

6. The great river about eighty miles west of Tobacco Plains would be the Kootenay River, after it returns to Canada near Creston, British Columbia.

7. About 1870 Father Grassi visited the Cranbrook area Kootenai band and had a similar greeting: "We found all the Indians drawn up in a double line in the centre of the village, waiting to shake hands with the Missioner; which ceremony assumes with them a religious character, beginning and ending with the sign of the cross." Grassi, 306–7.

8. No further information was located about this member of the Cranbrook Kootenai band. The missionaries had a special interest in these survival stories. Father Grassi reported meeting survivors of a bear at-

tack and a Blackfeet scalping while visiting the Tobacco Plains Kootenai band in the early 1870s. Grassi, 310–11.

9. After returning to St. Ignatius, Rappagliosi and Bandini reported to an unnamed priest, presumably Joseph Giorda, S.J., the superior general of the Rocky Mountain Mission: "I believe the Oblate fathers will thank your Reverence for that portion of the vineyard that you let them have. While we were at Joseph's camp, we heard that an Oblate father arrived at Abraham's camp. In those same days he gathered there all the chiefs, Abraham, Joseph, Moses, David, to decide where the Church can be built. It's clear that everyone will speak for their own place. Having heard such news we hastened to get out of there, reluctantly declining to visit another camp of the Siguepi who had come to summon us. All we could do was to say that soon another black robe will console them." The Oblate priest would have been Leon Fouquet, O.M.I., who established St. Eugene Mission near Cranbrook in 1874 and was in charge until 1887. Rappagliosi and J. Bandini to "Reverend in Christ Father," Aug. 30, 1874, Joseph Bandini File, OPA; Smyth, 70–71; Kay Cronin, *Cross in the Wilderness* (Vancouver BC: Mitchell, 1960), 136, 202.

10. The Signeses were probably the Salish-speaking Lakes Indians, who lived in the area around the Arrow Lakes and Kettle River in British Columbia and Washington. This small tribe was just west of the Kootenay Lake area that Rappagliosi and Bandini were then visiting. Other sources give their name as the Senijextee or sna'itckstk tribe. One of their principal sources of support was the salmon fishery at Kettle Falls, which they shared with several neighboring tribes. No information was found about their chief Paul Ignatius. Verne F. Ray, "Native Villages and Groupings of the Columbia Basin," *Pacific Northwest Quarterly* 27, no. 2 (Apr. 1936): 99–152; Robert H. Ruby and John A. Brown, *A Guide to the Indian Tribes of the Pacific Northwest*, rev. ed. (Norman: University of Oklahoma Press, 1992), 188–89; David H. Chance, *People of the Falls* (n.p.: Kettle Falls Historical Center, 1986).

11. Bandini, wrote later that Rappagliosi "wasn't accustomed to traveling in the rain, nor to sleeping on the ground, especially being so wet. . . . On the return home after more than a month, Father Rappagliosi's pants, which were not of great quality, ripped, and in the morning he stitched them on the bank of the river without complaining, and he said smiling: 'What would my mother say to me if she saw me doing this?'" *Memorie*, 17.

18. HARDSHIPS OF WINTER

1. Lucca is a city in northwestern Italy.
2. The *Weekly Missoulian* in nearby Missoula lamented on February 10, 1875: "Will it never let up? When it don't [*sic*] snow every day, it makes up by snowing three times a day for the next week. We've determined not to dispose of our snow shoes until the first day of next August." Other issues carried news of serious stock losses from the severe winter. *wm*, Feb. 10, 1875, p. 3, col. 1; Mar. 24, 1875, p. 3, col. 3; and Apr. 7, 1875, p. 2, col. 4.
3. The man who died was Moses Koitó; see appendix C.

19. DEATH OF A YOUNG INDIAN

1. The post office closest to St. Ignatius was at Missoula, Montana Territory.
2. The young married man who died was Peter Andrew; see appendix C.

20. DEALINGS WITH AN INDIAN CHIEF

This letter was originally published in German in *Katholischen Missionen* (Freiburg, Germany) 4 (1876): 173–74. The first sentence of the 1876 introduction refers to an undated letter that Rappagliosi wrote while at St. Mary's and that was published in *Katholischen Missionen* 4 (1876): 154–55. The earlier letter duplicates material in other letters in the *Memorie*, so it has not been reprinted in the present edition. Rappagliosi probably wrote these letters to someone other than his parents, who received most of the letters in the *Memorie*.

1. The Indian camp to which Rappagliosi refers would be the camp of Chief Arlee's band of Salish Flatheads, who had removed from the Bitterroot Valley to the Jocko Valley in 1873.
2. One of the women was probably Arlee's second wife, Mary, half Salish and half Iroquois, whose Indian name was Kwikwita. Her birth date is uncertain, but she died in 1912. The other woman could have been Arlee's oldest daughter, Christine, who was about twelve in 1875. Arlee also had at least four sons who were still alive in 1886, when the first census was taken. According to Mary Ronan three of Arlee's sons

were killed fighting the Crows and Blackfeet. Eugene Mark Felsman, "Flathead Indian Reservation Genealogy Files" (Polson, Mont.), entries for Chief Arlee and family; U.S. Bureau of Indian Affairs, *Indian Census Rolls, 1885–1940,* NAmf M595, reel 107, frames 59–60, 139, 227–28; Ronan, 125–26.

21. DEVOTION OF THE INDIANS TO HOLY MARY

1. In June 1875, Rappagliosi stopped in Helena while on his way to St. Peter's Mission among the Blackfeet. At six A.M. on June 27, he delivered a sermon in Salish to a large number of Flathead Indians in the Helena Catholic church. "The Indians Attend Church," *Helena Daily Herald,* June 28, 1875, p. 3, col. 1.

22. ST. PETER'S MISSION AT THE BLACKFEET

1. Fort Shaw, an army post near the mouth of the Sun River on the road between Helena and Fort Benton, was established in 1867. Don Miller and Stan Cohen, *Military & Trading Posts of Montana* (Missoula MT: Pictorial Histories Publishing, 1978), 76–82.

23. INDIANS' WAYS OF LIFE AND SUPERSTITIONS

1. The original of this sentence is flawed. One word is missing, and the construction is incomplete. – Trans.

24. RELIGIOUS INSTRUCTION AND THE LIFE OF MISSIONARIES

1. Rappagliosi is probably referring to the party of twenty-two lodges of Pend d'Oreilles Indians who came on the Blackfeet Reservation (which then covered much of northern Montana) to hunt in July 1875. White Calf, a Piegan subchief, gave his reluctant consent, provided it was a one-time affair. The Blackfeet agent complained in October 1875 about conflict between the tribes concentrated to hunt the shrinking buffalo herds. The Pend d'Oreilles had to leave the Blackfeet Reservation quickly at the end of October after some young Pend d'Oreilles men

lassoed the wife and daughter of Little Plume, the Blackfeet chief. U.S. Indian Agent to Commanding Officer, Fort Shaw, Mont., Oct. 8, 1875, vol. 1, copies of general letters sent, June 1875-June 1915, Blackfeet Agency Papers, Bureau of Indian Affairs, RG 75, National Archives – Rocky Mountain Division, Denver CO; "Indian Troubles," *Helena Independent*, Nov. 5, 1875, p. 3, col. 3.

2. The river Rappagliosi mentions is the Two Medicine River in the Marias River drainage of north-central Montana.

3. The editor was unable to locate further information about the Piegan Indian named Orkonnokim.

25. LETTER FROM PIUS IX

1. By 1875 Pope Pius IX had lost control of Rome to the Italian Republic and was a voluntary prisoner in the Vatican. The letter from the pope is in response to a letter from the Salish Indians at St. Ignatius expressing their sympathy for his situation and their loyalty and devotion to him. According to Father Palladino, when the return letter arrived at St. Ignatius, messengers were sent in every direction to gather the Indian community, and when large numbers had assembled at St. Ignatius: "The Papal Brief was read in Flat Head [sic], Kootenay, and English, the words of the Holy Father being listened to with profound reverence and breathless attention and sinking deep into their hearts. The event was one never to be forgotten, and may be said to have marked a new era for our work among the Indians." Palladino, 170–72. A copy of the original letter to Rome in Salish and the pope's response in Latin are reproduced in *pntmc*, reel 4, frames 377–85.

2. Father Scellen is Constantine Scollen, O.M.I.; see appendix C.

3. The Oblates of Mary Immaculate (O.M.I.) were a congregation of religious men founded in France in 1816. Among many other activities, they had been very active as missionaries to Indian and Eskimo communities in western Canada, including the Canadian Blackfeet and Métis. *New Catholic Encyclopedia*, 1967 ed., s.v. "Oblates of Mary Immaculate."

26. MISSION WORK AMONG THE INDIANS

This letter was originally published in German in *Katholischen Missionen* (Freiburg, Germany) 4 (1876): 197–98. Evidence within the letter indicates that it was written to someone other than Rappagliosi's parents, who received most of the letters in the *Memorie*.

1. See letter 24, written January 3, 1876, in which Rappagliosi refers to meeting fifteen lodges of Pend d'Oreilles Indians in December 1875. Presumably the lodges he mentions here were part of the Pend d'Oreilles hunting party that came on the Blackfeet Reservation in July 1875 and was discussed in letter 24. In that letter, written from Old Fort Maginnis on the Two Medicine River, Rappagliosi identifies the site of Arsapaki's camp as on Two Medicine River, which drains the southern Blackfeet Indian Reservation and forms the Marias River south of Cut Bank, Montana. Two Medicine Creek was also called Mátoki Okás or Two Medicine Lodges River. James Willard Schultz, *Blackfeet and Buffalo: Memories of Life among the Indians*, ed. Keith C. Seele (Norman: University of Oklahoma Press, 1962), 376.
2. The Orso River could not be identified.
3. St. Alphons is St. Alphonsus Liguori; see appendix C.
4. This boy is the son of Three Chiefs; see appendix C.

27. CHILDREN'S BAPTISMS AMONG THE INDIANS

1. The Badger River refers to Badger Creek in southern Glacier County, which flows into Two Medicine River.
2. In the next letter Rappagliosi indicates that the elderly Kootenai he refers to here is named Baptiste.
3. The Assiniboines were a Siouan-speaking tribe whose home territory was east of the Blackfeet. They were traditional enemies of the Blackfeet and Sioux tribes. In the 1870s when the diminishing buffalo herds were pulling the Plains tribes into closer contact, the Assiniboines were hunting the same buffalo herds as the Blackfeet and Sioux. With increased intertribal warfare and decreased resources, the tribes attempted to make peace. James Larpenteur Long, *The Assiniboines: From the Accounts of the Old Ones Told to First Boy (James Larpenteur Long)*, ed. Michael Stephen Kennedy (Norman: University of Oklahoma Press, 1961), xix–lix; McGinnis, *Counting Coup*, 129–71.

28. APOSTOLIC WORKS AT ST. PETER'S MISSION

1. In a letter of February 9, 1877, Rappagliosi indicated that the camp on the Marias River included Piegan, Blood, Gros Ventres, Pend d'Oreilles, Coeur d'Alene, Flathead, and Spokane Indians totaling three hundred lodges. He reported baptizing 104 children. "Missionary Work among the Indians," *Helena Independent,* Feb 23, 1877, p. 3. col. 3.
2. The Spokanes were a Salish tribe who lived in what is now eastern Washington. Their villages were mostly along the Little Spokane River and the Spokane River below Spokane Falls. Their language and culture were very similar to those of the Salish Flatheads and Pend d'Oreilles Father Rappagliosi knew from St. Mary's and St. Ignatius. The salmon were much more important than the buffalo for this tribe, but many families had close ties to their Pend d'Oreilles neighbors and joined in their buffalo hunts. Robert H. Ruby and John A. Brown, *The Spokane Indians: Children of the Sun* (Norman: University of Oklahoma Press, 1970); Teit.
3. *"Adesto fideles"* refers to *Adeste Fideles,* the Latin version of *O Come All Ye Faithful.* The Kyrie is the "Lord Have Mercy," the only Greek part of the Latin Mass.
4. The *scudo* was an Italian coin approximately equivalent to a dollar.

29. ON THE DEATH OF HIS BROTHER LUIGI

1. This letter was written by Father Philip when he heard of the news of his brother Luigi's death, who was twenty-five years old when his wife and parents lost him in a few days to a violent illness. – 1879 editor.

30. THE ENCAMPMENT OF THE MÉTIS

1. "Bufford" is Fort Buford, North Dakota, a U.S. Army post between 1866 and 1894. It was located at the junction of the Missouri and Yellowstone Rivers near the old Fort Union trading post, close to the Montana border. In 1881 Sitting Bull surrendered there. Usher L. Burdick, *Tales From Buffalo Land: The Story of Fort Buford* (Baltimore MD: Wirth Brothers, 1940).
2. Father Jean Baptiste Genin, O.M.I., who spent the winter of 1877–78 among these Métis described their reception of priests: "On his [the

priest's] arrival at the camp he would meet the good people standing in two rows on each side of his passage, with the children in front of them as if protected by the innocence of the latter, they would dare to face the minister of Christ. All would fall on their knees, and the young men fire their guns, whilst the priest was giving them his blessing." Slaughter, 1:236.

3. The *Graduale Romanum* was a liturgical book containing the chants incorporated in the Mass. Nevins, *Maryknoll Catholic Dictionary*, 256.

4. The Cypress Hills are in southwestern Saskatchewan, about eighty miles north of the present site of Havre, Montana.

31. ON THE DEATH OF HIS BROTHER STANISLAO

1. He speaks here of his other brother Stanislao who at the age of eighteen died of a slow illness in the kiss of God one and a half months after Luigi's death. – 1879 editor.

2. Rappagliosi refers to the Battle of the Bear Paws, which climaxed a brilliant seventeen-hundred-mile retreat through Idaho, Montana, and Wyoming by about 750 Nez Perce during the Nez Perce War of 1877. The battle took place about fifteen miles south of the present site of Chinook, Montana, between September 30 and October 5, 1877. The Nez Perce prisoners had left Fort Benton on October 8. Alvin M. Josephy Jr., *The Nez Perce Indians and the Opening of the Northwest* (New Haven CT: Yale University Press, 1965), 616–33.

33. DEPARTURE FOR THE LAST MISSION

1. This account was never written because about a month later, as narrated in the first section, while at the Métis camp, Father Philip was called unto God. This letter, written to one of his surviving brothers, was the last one that he sent from the Rocky Mountains to Europe. – 1879 editor.

APPENDIX A

This biography was published in *Woodstock Letters* 8 no. 2 (1879): 97–109 as an obituary for Rappagliosi. The author, Father Joseph Guidi, S.J., was at St. Peter's with Rappagliosi and had been a friend of Rappagliosi's in Europe. A slightly longer version of the biography was published in the Memorie, 9–31. The editor has omitted the first two pages covering Rappagliosi's early life and his training as a Jesuit. The spelling has been modernized.

1. The gestures were usually referred to as Indian sign language, which was widely used on the Great Plains.

2. The father who wrote this was Joseph Bandini, S.J. Memorie, 16.

3. The tribal chief was probably Michelle, the Pend d'Oreilles chief. According to the Memorie, the chief talked to the superior general, not the superior of the St. Ignatius Mission. The superior general of the Rocky Mountain Mission from 1862 to 1866 and 1869 to 1877 was Joseph Giorda, S.J. Memorie, 16; Bischoff, 222.

   During the 1870s the Pend d'Oreilles maintained a jail at St. Ignatius and a volunteer police force under the supervision of Andre, the second chief of the Pend d'Oreilles. The jail had only one room, which turned out to be a problem when a couple were arrested for adultery in 1878. In the Memorie Guidi described Rappagliosi's efforts to help prisoners in the jail at St. Ignatius. While visiting and consoling the prisoners he noticed that they were suffering from the cold. He approached the superior general, Father Giorda, about supplying warm clothing, but Giorda declined because the mission was already responsible for feeding the prisoners. Giorda thought the local Indian community should provide for the prisoners. Rappagliosi went from door to door until he secured the necessary clothing. Memorie, 17–18; Peter Ronan to CIA, Aug. 13, 1877, arsi, 1877, 532; "The Indian Side of the Question," wm, Apr. 12, 1878, p. 3, col. 3–4.

4. One family that lived near St. Peter's Mission was that of Edward A. Lewis, a white man who married a daughter of Meek-i-appy (Heavy Shield) or Cut-Hands, a Piegan war chief. Mrs. Lewis was a baptized Christian. Their marriage was performed by Father Imoda in 1869. Robert Vaughn, Then and Now; or, Thirty-Six Years in the Rockies (Minneapolis MN: Tribune Printing, 1900), 130–31.

5. The encampments mentioned here were small trading posts established by white traders in northern Montana.

6. The decline in the buffalo herds made hunting more unpredictable in 1877, but other reports do not indicate widespread starvation among

the Blackfeet at this time. In the 1880s, however, mass starvation haunted the Blackfeet with the extinction of the buffalo. John Young to CIA, June 14, 1878, NAmf234, reel 512, frames 604-7; John S. Wood to CIA, Aug. 25, 1876, arsi, 1876, 489-91; Ewers, The Blackfeet, 277-96.

7. In the 1870s Fort Belknap was an Indian agency on the south side of the Milk River opposite the present site of Chinook. In 1888 the fort was moved twenty-five miles to its present location southeast of Harlem. Miller and Cohen, Military & Trading Posts of Montana, 10-11.

8. Fort Benton, on the Missouri River about forty miles northeast of the present site of Great Falls, was the steamboat port farthest up the Missouri River. Until the railroad was completed through Montana in the 1880s, Fort Benton was a key transport and shipping center for Montana Territory. During the 1870s it was the source of whiskey for the Whoop Up Trail that supplied whiskey traders in southern Alberta. It was also the location of a U.S. Army post during the 1870s. Joel Overhosler, Fort Benton: World's Innermost Port (Fort Benton MT: privately published, 1987).

    The Benton Record noted in January 1878: "Fathers Imoda and Rappagliosi were in town during the holidays. These clergymen are careful of the spiritual welfare of our Catholic population." Fort Benton Record, Jan. 11, 1878, p. 3, col. 1.

9. The doctor would have been among the Métis camped in the Wood Mountain area of south-central Saskatchewan. As the following paragraphs of the biography indicate, Father Decorby was also living in the Wood Mountain area during the winter of 1877-78. Marcel Giraud, The Metis in the Canadian West (Lincoln: University of Nebraska Press, 1986), 2:403.

10. In the biographical sketch in the Memorie, Guidi mentions that Capt. Constant Williams of the U.S. Army was also present when Rappagliosi died. He was returning from issuing annuities to the Gros Ventres. Memorie, 28.

11. In 1920 Rappagliosi's body was moved to Mount St. Michael's Cemetery north of Spokane, Washington. Wilfred P. Schoenberg, S.J., Paths to the Northwest: A Jesuit History of the Oregon Province (Chicago: Loyola University Press, 1982), 321.

APPENDIX B

1. See original photographs in OPA (number 1027.02) and Montana Historical Society Photographic Archives (number 943-755), Helena, Montana. The Montana Historical Society Photographic Archives has documentation on the photographic work of Eckert and Bundy in Montana. The Bundy photo can be found in L. B. Palladino, S.J., *Indian and White in the Northwest; or, A History of Catholicity in Montana* (Baltimore MD: John Murphy, 1894), 188.

2. C. Imoda, S.J., to Rev. in Christ Father Superior, Mar. 4, 1878, Philip Rappagliosi file, OPA.

3. Palladino, 219.

4. "Father Genin," *nyfj*, Jan. 12, 1878, p. 1, col. 4-5; [Father Genin's Letter], *nyfj*, Sept. 14, 1878, p. 4, col. 4-5, and Sept. 21, 1878, p. 4, col. 4-5.

5. Slaughter; Carrière, 2:80.

6. Oblates of Mary Immaculate, "Proces Verbaux des deliberations du Conseil General de la Congregation des Oblats de Marie Immaculee a partir du ler Janvier 1873 (au 30 decembre 1878)," p. 217, entry for Sept. 8, 1876, Archives, Oblates of Mary Immaculate, Rome, Italy; J. B. M. Genin, O.M.I., to Rev. Father Martinet, O.M.I., Nov. 21, 1876, Archives, Oblates of Mary Immaculate, Rome, Italy; Carrière, 2:80.

7. "Father Genin," *nyfj*, Jan. 12, 1878, p. 1, col. 4-5; [Father Genin's Letter], *nyfj*, Sept. 14, 1878, p. 4, col. 4-5, and Sept. 21, 1878, p. 4, col. 4-5.

8. "Father Genin," *nyfj*, Jan. 12, 1878, p. 1, col. 4-5.

9. C. Imoda, S.J., to Rev. in Christ Father Superior, Mar. 4, 1878, Philip Rappagliosi file, OPA.

10. Henry Brooks to Rev. Father Palladino, Mar. 6, 1878, Philip Rappagliosi file, OPA.

11. The Holy Viaticum is the Holy Eucharist as given to a person in danger of dying.

12. *Memorie*, 48-50.

13. Palladino, 218-19; *Who Was Who in America* (Chicago: A. N. Marquis, 1943), 1:852; NAmf666, reel 294, file 4408 AGO 1876 (see especially frames 717-40) and reel 362, file 4976 AGO 1877 (see especially frames 114-29, 193-97, and 216-17).

APPENDIX C

1. "Kootenay Chiefs," folder 57, Claude Schaeffer Papers, Glenbow-Alberta Foundation, Calgary, Alberta.

2. L. B. Palladino, S.J., "Founders of the Flathead Mission and Some of Their Successors," *Indian Sentinel* (Washington DC) 1, no. 14 (Oct. 1919): 18–27; Palladino, 82–83; "St. Mary's Mission, Montana, 'Liber Mortuorum,' 1866–1893," pntmc, reel 1, frame 186.

3. "Liber Defunctorum, 1874–1898," St. Ignatius Mission, St. Ignatius MT, 4.

4. O'Connor, 104–5; Ronan, 125–26; George G. Vest and Martin Maginnis, "Report of the Subcommittee of the Special Committee of the United States Senate Appointed to Visit the Indian Tribes in Northern Montana," 48th Cong., 1st sess., 1884, Sen. Rept. No. 283, serial 2174, xiv.

5. Mendizábal, 169, #9,386; *Catalogus, 1874–76;* Wilfred P. Schoenberg, S.J., *A Chronicle of the Catholic History of the Pacific Northwest, 1743–1960* (Spokane WA: Gonzaga Preparatory School, 1962), 126, 163; "Father Bendini [sic] Dead," *Spokane WA Spokesman-Review,* Feb. 12, 1899, p. 8, col. 4.

6. J. W. Schultz, *My Life as an Indian* (New York: Doubleday, Page, 1907), 121–33.

7. *Encyclopedia Britannica,* 11th ed., s.v. "Beckx, Pierre Jean."

8. "A Pioneer: Governor Brooks, One of the Best Known Men in State Dies at Lewistown," *Great Falls* MT *Daily Tribune,* Feb. 26, 1909, p. 1, col. 7.

9. Palladino, 85–90; Dusenberry, "Samples of Pend d'Oreille Oral Literature," 109–20; Ronan, 145–53.

10. Davis, *History of St. Ignatius Mission,* 122–23.

11. Smyth, 67; P. O'Reilly to Superintendent-General of Indian Affairs, Dec. 16, 1884, *Annual Report of the Department of Indian Affairs,* Canada Parliament, Sessional Paper No. 3, 1885, lxxiii–lxxv; Kootenai Indian Tribe, Tobacco Plains Band, "Statement of Members of Tobacco Plains Band, Kootenai Tribe Re Setting Aside of Reserves by Judge O'Reilly," SC 645, Montana Historical Society Archives, Helena MT; Michael Phillips to Superintendent-General of Indian Affairs, June 30, 1892, *Annual Report of the Department of Indian Affairs,* Canada Parliament, Sessional Paper No. 14, 1893, 245–47.

12. Carrière, 1:260.

13. E. Laveille, S.J., *The Life of Father De Smet, S.J., (1801–1873)* (1915; reprint,

Chicago: Loyola University Press, 1981); Carriker, *Father Peter John De Smet*.

14. Alexander Diomedi, S.J., *Sketches of Indian Life in the Pacific Northwest* (Fairfield WA: Ye Galleon Press, 1978), 7-9; Bischoff, 219-20.

15. Bischoff, 222.

16. John C. Ewers, letter to Bigart, April 14, 1994; John S. Wood to CIA, Sept. 25, 1975, *arsi*, 1875, 801-3.

17. Bischoff, 223-24.

18. *Catalogus*, 1873-99; [Guidi], "Obituary: Father Philip Rappagliosi"; "Father Guidi in Brazil," *Anaconda* MT *Standard*, Nov. 14, 1899, p. 16, col. 2; "All Over the State," *Missoulian*, Feb. 15, 1902, p. 3, col. 3-4; Mendizábal, 211, #11,703; Palladino, 72, 160, 478; Wilfred P. Schoenberg, S.J., *Jesuit Mission Presses in the Pacific Northwest* (Portland OR: Champoeg Press, 1957), 18-21.

19. Turney-High, *Ethnography of the Kutenai*, 14-21; Ronan, 124-25; O'Connor, 104.

20. Bischoff, 224.

21. David McLaughlin, "A Short History of the Lower Kootenai Indians," Aug. 20, 1884, MONAC Collection, MS 184, box 24, Eastern Washington State Historical Society, Spokane WA; Charles Wilson, "Report on the Indian Tribes Inhabiting the Country in the Vicinity of the 49th Parallel of North Latitude," *Transactions of the Ethnological Society of London* 4 (1866): 305; R. L. T. Galbraith, "A Glance Back Thirty Years," *Cranbrook* BC *Herald*, Dec. 1904, Christmas edition, unpaged; Clara Graham, *Fur and Gold in the Kootenays* (Vancouver BC: Wrigley Printing, 1945), 162.

22. "Liber Defunctorum, 1874-1898," St. Ignatius Mission, St. Ignatius MT, 4.

23. Mendizábal, 188, #10,434; *Catalogus*, 1879-80; Sister Genevieve McBride, O.S.U., *The Bird Tail* (New York: Vantage, 1974), 17.

24. John C. Ewers, letter to Bigart, April 14, 1994; John S. Wood to CIA, Sept. 25, 1875, ARSI, 1875, 801-3; Andrew Dusold to Col. R. F. May, Mar. 1, 1874, NAmf234, reel 499, frames 603-5; R. F. May to CIA, Mar. 24, 1874, NAmf234, reel 499, frames 606-7; Robert W. Lind, *Brother Van: Montana Pioneer Circuit Rider* (Helena MT: Falcon, 1992), 166-73.

25. Mendizábal, 94, #5,220; *Catalogus*, 1874-76.

26. John C. Ewers, *Gustavus Sohon's Portraits of Flathead and Pend d' Oreille Indians, 1854*, Smithsonian Miscellaneous Collections, 110, no. 7 (Wash

ington DC, 1948), 50–52; "Old Cheif [sic] Michel," *Daily Missoulian*, May 14, 1897, p. 1, col. 3.

27. Galbraith, "Glance Back Thirty Years"; Graham, *Fur and Gold in the Kootenays*, 168–74.

28. Mendizábal, 232, #12,888; *Catalogus*, 1875–89; "John Negro Dead," *Lewiston* ID *Morning Tribune*, Dec. 17, 1912, p. 6.

29. Mendizábal, 208, #11,543.

30. Augustin de Backer, *Bibliotheque de la Compagnie de Jesus*, new ed. (Brussels and Paris: Oscar Schepens and Alphonse Picard, 1890–1909), 6:1387–88.

31. *Encyclopedia Canadiana*, 1977 ed., s.v. "Scollen, Constantine"; Carrière, 3:178–79.

32. "St. Mary's Mission, Montana, 'Liber Mortuorum,' 1866–1893," PNTMC, reel 1, frame 191.

33. U.S. Bureau of Indian Affairs, *Indian Census Rolls, 1885–1940*, NAmf M595, reel 3, frames 22, 71, 121, 158; Blackfeet Heritage Program, *Blackfeet Heritage, 1907–1908: Blackfeet Indian Reservation, Browning Montana* (Browning MT: Blackfeet Heritage Program, [1980?]), 96, 270, 280.

34. U.S. Census Office, *Tenth Census of the United States, 1880*, NAmf T9, reel 742, Montana, Meagher County, Judith Basin, ED 23, p. 4, lines 41–46; Howard, *Strange Empire*, 344.

35. Capt. Constant Williams to Acting Asst. Adjutant General, District of Montana, Feb. 6, 1878, NAmf666, reel 362, frames 114–24; *Records of Living Officers of the United States Army* (Philadelphia PA: L. R. Hamersly, 1884), 264–65; *Who Was Who in America* (Chicago: A. N. Marquis, 1943), 1:1350.

Index

Numbers in italics refer to the photographic insert; the first number is that of the text page preceding the insert, the second is that of the page of the insert.

of, 35, 56-51, 56-52, 99-100; piety
of, 90; and priestly calling, 1-2; and
St. Ignatius Mission, 51-60; and
St. Mary's Mission, 24-45; and St.
Peter's Mission, 60-88; and travel to
St. Mary's, 7-24
Rappagliosi, Stanislao, 79, 84-85, 136 n.1
religion: Piegan, 63
Roettger, Mr., 12
rosary: Métis, 82; Piegan, 71

Salish Flathead Indians, xviii-xix, xxi-
xxv, 24-45, 89, 98; baptisms of, 38, 127
n.7; and beards, 27; buffalo hunts
and, 29, 31; and catechism, 28, 35-
36; confessions of, 33; costume of,
32; and death feasts, 38-39, 127-28
n.8; deaths of, 37-38; and fishing, 35;
and gifting, 43; and horsemanship,
29-30; hospitality of, 43-44; houses
of, 32; icons of, 32-33; piety of, xxxii;
and sewing, 44-45; and smoking, 39,
43-44; and tepees, 25, 125 n.3; visiting customs of, 42-44; and worship,
24-25. See also Jocko Valley Salish
Flathead Indians; St. Mary's Mission
Salish Indian language, 24-25, 27-28,
35-36, 41, 56, 89, 111-12
Scellen, Constantine, O.M.I. See
Scollen, Constantine, O.M.I.
schools: at St. Ignatius Mission, xxix,
73, 108
Scollen, Constantine, O.M.I., 67, 115
sewing: and Salish Flatheads, 44-45
Shanahan, Charles, xxix
Signeses Indians, 51, 130 n.10
sign language, 29, 89
singing: St. Mary's Mission, 31
Sioux Indians, 101
Sisters of Charity of Providence, 34
Sitting Bull (Sioux Chief), 101-2

smoking: and Jocko Valley Salish
Flatheads, 56-57; and Salish Flatheads, 39, 43-44; and Tobacco Plains
Kootenais, 48
Snake Indians, 29, 126 n.3
Society of Jesus, 92
Spokane Indians, 135 n.2; baptisms of,
76; confessions of, 76
stagecoach travel, 21-23
starvation, Piegan, 93, 137-38 n.6
St. Francis Regis Mission (WA). See Fort
Colville
St. Ignatius Mission, xxvii, xxx-xxxii,
27, 56-5, 98, 133 n.1; and catechism,
54; Christmas at, 57; and communion, 46, 57; feast of St. Ignatius
at, 46; jail of, 137 n.3; and letter
from Pope, 67-69; Rappagliosi at,
46, 51-60, 90; schools at, xxix, 73,
108; and Virgin Mary, 58-59; and
winter weather, 51-53. See also Pend
d'Oreilles Indians
St. Mary's Mission, xviii, xxv-xxvii,
56-4, 98; and beards, 27; and bed-
ding, 45; and beverages, 34; and
costume, 44-45; and diet, 34, 45; and
Easter season, 31-32; Easter Sunday
at, 31-32; Good Friday service at,
31; Rappagliosi at, 24-45, 89; and
singing, 31; visiting parishioners
of, 32-33. See also Salish Flathead
Indians
St. Peter's Mission, xxxv-xxxvi, 56-6,
97, 111; and mass, 91; Rappagliosi at,
60-88, 90-91; and winter weather,
67. See also Piegan Indians
Suzanna (Salish Flathead), 37-39, 115

tepees: Piegan, 65; Salish Flathead, 25,
125 n.3
Three Chiefs (Piegan), 72, 115

Lightning Source UK Ltd.
Milton Keynes UK
UKOW03f1242160414

230075UK00004B/230/P